Bogie

A Celebration of the Life
and Films of Humphrey Bogart

Foreword by Stephen Bogart
Appreciation by Richard Schickel
The Movies by George Perry

Aurum

First published in the United Kingdom in 2006 by

Aurum Press Ltd
25 Bedford Avenue
London
WC1B 3AT

Created and produced for Aurum Press Ltd by

Palazzo Editions Limited
15 Gay Street
Bath, BA1 2PH
United Kingdom
www.palazzoeditions.com

Designed by Peter Whitehead and Richard Chant.

ISBN-10 1 84513 206 8
ISBN-13 978 1 84513 206 4

Printed and bound in Singapore.

Contents

Foreword by Stephen Bogart

When I think of my father today he is much fuller to me than the man I barely knew. He died when I was only eight years old, just as we were beginning to connect in that special father-son way. His death of course changed my life forever, but I'm writing this on Father's Day and I'm thinking about the pieces of him I've put together over the years. In the years after he died I realized he was the greatest star of his time, but for years thereafter I careened through life not only knowing how much I really missed just having a father, but also not realizing who he really was as a man. I mean, who was this regular guy who was to become an icon of the twentieth and now the twenty-first century, who just had the street where he was born in New York City named after him, "Humphrey Bogart Place"?

Most people regard him as that icon. A tremendous actor, a world-class sailor, a champion chess player, a six-handicap golfer and a proud Navy man in World War 1.

He was privileged, yes, the son of a doctor and a successful artist … never had to worry much about money, attended good schools … but he always seemed to rebel against that. He didn't want to be treated differently because he got lucky in the birth lottery. He felt he was no better than anyone else and that's how he lived his life. He was a leader, a trailblazer, a man who stood up for what he believed in, both in the way he thought and what he did.

In the early 1940s he came out in support of FDR and got tons of hate mail. In the late 1940s he and his great friend John Huston led a group of actors (including my mother) and writers, dubbed by the press "The Unfriendly Ten," to Washington to protest Congress's desperate search for communists in the movie industry. This was three years before old Joe McCarthy even got started. My father risked his reputation, his career, everything. But he stood up against the hysteria of the times for what he believed in.

He was also among the first true Hollywood stars to start his own production company and begin the break from the old studio system. He was the highest

Bogie and Bacall
An off-set studio portrait by Warner during
the filming of *Dark Passage* (1947).

paid star of this time, but he didn't sit on that … he took a chance and formed Santana Productions. Santana made four films before he died, including *The African Queen*, which won him a Best Actor Oscar. Before that he had pushed and prodded—sometimes none too gently—Jack Warner, to let him do the kinds of movies and play the types of roles he thought would make him better, leading to him being among the first Hollywood stars to break away from the whole studio system. He wanted to branch out as an actor and move away from being forever remembered as a quintessential gangster. He wanted to be the quintessential actor.

But it takes more than all that to transform into the beloved icon that he is, and he had it.

He was a very smart man, very well-read, as was the customary definition of "intelligent" before the computer age came to replace all that. He struck a chord with men and women alike. There was simply a certain truth in the way he lived his life. He hated the whole "movie star" thing. He wanted to be treated like anyone else, and he treated everyone the same. He was a family man and a man who you'd love to sit down with and have a few drinks. He was true to his friends the way that only men are, and he treated women with love and respect.

I guess when you put it all together, he stood for a bit of what each of us wants in our lives, especially in these difficult times when there is divisiveness here at home and abroad. It's the battle for individual freedom we in America have

"Nobody likes me on sight. I suppose that's why I'm cast as the heavy."

Humphrey Bogart

His Two Loves
Bogart, with Bacall, under sail, his other passion, off the Southern California coast.

fought for more than 230 years to date…. It's the freedom, individual freedom, to do what we want as long as it doesn't hurt anyone else. My father believed in the old Golden Rule. He lived his life that way and he also treated others in that way, and the people loved and still love him for it. His was a total honesty, right there on the table, in your face, and that appealed to just about everyone.

He had a piece of every one of us in him, yet he was unique to every one who knew him. To all of his close friends, colleagues, associates, and acquaintances, and the millions more who loved and still love him, his great friend, the genius director John Huston, put it best in his eulogy, "There will never be another like him."

"He loved to argue. When he and Mom lived in the farmhouse in Benedict Canyon she put up a sign that said:

DANGER: BOGART AT WORK. DO NOT DISCUSS POLITICS, RELIGION, WOMEN, MEN, PICTURES, THEATRE, OR ANYTHING ELSE

Bogie seemed to bask in his role as a troublemaker."

Stephen Bogart, *Bogart: In Search of my Father*

At Home with the Bogarts
Bogie and Bacall with their two children, Leslie Howard and Stephen Humphrey. "I was named Stephen after the character my father played in *To Have and Have Not*, the film that brought my mother and father together," Stephen Bogart.

Following Pages **Farewell to Stephen**
The Bogarts in the Jaguar roadster are leaving their son at home at Mapleton Drive.

The Genuine Article by Richard Schickel

We'll always have *Casablanca*. More important, *he'll* always have *Casablanca*. For every star needs to have at least one film that transcends the moment of its making, asserts its continuing claims on generations unborn when it first appeared. Without a film of seemingly endless popular appeal in their resumes, movie stars, no matter how powerful their presence appears to be when they are in their ascendancy, tend, over the years, to retreat into the shadows of cable television, cultish regard and vaguely approving nostalgia.

This movie may or may not represent the best work of these stars. The knowing cinephile may prefer James Stewart in *Vertigo* instead of *It's a Wonderful Life*, James Cagney in *White Heat* as opposed to *Yankee Doodle Dandy*, Cary Grant in *The Awful Truth* not *An Affair to Remember*, John Wayne in *The Searchers* rather than *True Grit*. I am not alone in thinking that Humphrey Bogart's masterpiece is *In a Lonely Place*, not *Casablanca*. But we have to face facts: If he had not played Rick Blaine it is doubtful that we would be gathered here to mark the 50th anniversary of his passing. Movie history, especially in its more popular forms, is like every other sort of cultural history; it hurries on, distracted and amnesiac, heeding certain inescapable benchmarks, but not the more subtle ebbs and flows of complex careers.

And Bogart's career was more complicated than most. To begin with, the longevity of his stardom was less than that of any of the other dominant male movie personalities of his era. It is true that he made his first movie in 1930, around the time that the stars with whom he must logically be compared—Astaire, Cagney, Cooper, Gable, Grant, Tracy, Wayne—did their first screen work. But he was not as quickly successful as most of them were, and he drifted back and forth between Broadway and Hollywood for some time before repeating his stage role as the gangster Duke Mantee, in the *The Petrified Forest*, for the cameras in 1936. It permitted him to establish Hollywood residence, but it did not permit him to establish full-scale stardom. He lurked about Warner Bros., playing the odd lead in minor movies, secondary roles in more important films, for another five years. In many of these pictures he was woefully miscast as a "tough guy," rather than what he essentially was—a romantic hiding his true nature under a gruff and sardonic shell. Whether you date his emergence as a figure to be reckoned with from *High Sierra* or *The Maltese Falcon* in 1941 or from *Casablanca* two years later, the fact is that he matched his own definition of stardom—"you have to drag your weight at the box office and be recognized wherever you go"—for a relatively short and belated period of time—less than two decades—before cancer prematurely claimed him in 1957.

Bogart was the first great figure of his generation of stars to go, and premature death always enhances, however briefly, a public figure's hold on his public, encouraged as they are by the cheap press to ponder sentimentally this highly visible evidence of life's mutability. But

Not Yet a Star
A self-conscious publicity pose after
signing his Warner contract in 1935.

Gary Cooper and Clark Gable died only a little later than he did, and also before their time, and they did not enjoy the strange, yet curiously rewarding, afterlife that Bogart did. This began in a rather odd, not to say exotic, place—with Jean-Luc Godard's *Breathless*, which appeared just three years after Bogart's death. In that curiously treasurable film, Jean-Paul Belmondo plays an ineffectual small-time criminal, yearning for something like Bogart's doomy romantic authority. At one point he and Jean Seberg, playing his inamorata, pause at a revival house, he glances up at a poster advertising one of the star's movies and wistfully sighs, "Ah, Bogie."

I don't know if Bogart's posthumous cult was born in that moment, or whether it reflects something that Godard sensed gathering in the air at the time, but more likely it was the latter, since *Breathless* was scarcely a mass-market hit. I don't think huge numbers of college students, anywhere in the world, saw it. What they did see, in *Casablanca* and elsewhere, was an unspoken, yet to them palpable, existentialist attitude that was a compound of dashed dreams and soured expectations that were nevertheless tinctured by a certain idealism which might still be reawakened by a good woman or a good idea. Somehow this figure suited the disaffected mood of disaffected youth—particularly among American college students—in the sixties.

They had more than *Casablanca* to go on. For however dismal Bogart's career had been up until the early forties, the years thereafter were more than kind to him: *To Have and Have Not*, *The Big Sleep*, *The Treasure of the Sierra Madre*, *In a Lonely Place*, as well as that wildly popular hit, *The African Queen* (which brought him the Oscar he deserved, but naturally for the wrong role, the Academy's voters always preferring to reward sweet sentiment rather than work with a harder edge). There were, indeed, other less remarked roles that were worthy of their attention—in *The Caine Mutiny*, in that delicious shaggy dog story, *Beat the Devil*, as the sardonic observer of *The Barefoot Contessa*. In a number of these films, he brought to the surface a raging paranoid anger—something ugly and dangerous that no other leading man I can think of so effectively tapped—that chimed persuasively with the inchoate anger that underlay the youth culture of the sixties.

About that, we will have more to say. For the moment it is sufficient for us to note that his appeal to "the kids" of the sixties granted him something no other actor has enjoyed in quite the same measure: An authentic second life. I believe that we make—or perhaps I should say we used to make—our strongest emotional connection with screen characters in our most impressionable years, roughly between the ages of ten and twenty, when the screen looms largest and more attractively in our lives, when we experience movies on our own recognizance, without "parental guidance" limiting our moviegoing experience. In a certain sense the actors and actresses we take to our hearts in that period are our first loves, thus in some sense our best loves. They are the figures that the passing years, our enhanced experience, can never quite talk us out of adoring. Bogart was, of course, such a figure for my generation, coming of age in the 1940s. But he alone of the great stars got a second chance, in the sixties, to enrapture a second generation.

It didn't last terribly long, this renewed enthusiasm. By the early seventies it was over and

The First Acclaimed Role
Humphrey Bogart as Duke Mantee in
The Petrified Forest (1935).

the next generation—the Jack Nicholsons and the Clint Eastwoods—began to assert their claims on youth. But it was not nothing. It was, in fact, unique in the history of cinema. It was also, I believe, a case of mistaken identity. I have already said that his first screen identity, as a "tough guy" was a misnomer. I also think that the notion of him as an existential hero, defining himself through actions at least in part made up for him by writers and directors, was equally a mistake. Bogart was an intelligent man and an actor who, when the opportunity presented itself, could draw on authentic emotions and attitudes to animate his best performances. But there is no evidence that he was any sort of intellectual, studying his Sartre or his Camus in order to shape his roles to fulfill the expectations of his devotees. The thought is thoroughly laughable.

I think Bogart's story is much simpler than that. I think it is the story of a displaced person, of a man born to a certain amount of wealth and privilege, somewhat rebellious—but not radically so—against the constraints of his upper-class beginnings who, through no fault of his own, found himself falling socially downward when he was quite a young man. He married three times, always unhappily, drank prodigiously, and always seemed to carry with him an air of regret, though for what it is hard to say: A lost life of upper-class ease? A more stable and private profession than acting? A solid, sustaining marriage? Some sense of ordinariness and anonymity that eluded him?

Impossible to say. All we know for certain is that his relationship to his profession—acting—was never more than, well, professional. We get no hints from any comments he made about it that he ever invested it with any great passion. It was, for him, a job of work. He groused from time to time about silly roles and studio stupidity, but he generally took the parts as they came, showed up on time to play them, getting along reasonably well with his directors and co-stars, then disappearing into the night for more boozing, which was conducted with the sober tenacity dedicated alcoholics bring to what is, finally, their only true vocation. The only avocation that claimed his regard was sailing, a lonely passion he had learned in his privileged youth and never abandoned.

From such record as we have of his private life we gain an impression of an old-school gentleman-idealist who never quite codified his ideals, but yet conveyed an air of regret over their betrayal—by himself, with his wastrel habits, by the world with the compromises it demanded. There was a mysterious ruefulness about the man long before, more or less by accident, the movies offered him ways of bringing that attitude to life on the screen. He was, in short, particularly in his own eyes, a man of breeding and privilege who found himself declassed as a result of circumstances not entirely of his making, far from his native haunts, among people of rather less quality, rather fewer standards morally, socially, intellectually than he had been raised to expect among his acquaintances. To put this matter concretely, Rick Blaine should not have ended up running a "gin joint" in *Casablanca*, and Humphrey Bogart should not have ended up being an actor in Hollywood. But that's the place he came

Smoke Screen
Bogart at the time of *In a Lonely Place* (1950), a part close to his true self.

to and his duty was to make the best of it as a kind of emotional remittance man, leading a life of privilege that, so far as he could tell, he had not earned and did not quite match, in his own mind certainly, the life of privilege he had inherited, but which had been squandered.

There had been inherited wealth to begin with—one of Bogart's grandfathers had invented a commercially successful process for engraving on tin—and both his parents had prospered in their careers. His father, Belmont de Forest Bogart, was a surgeon with an upper-echelon practice. His mother, Maud Humphrey Bogart, was a prominent commercial illustrator—she used her son as a model when he was a child—and also a militant suffragette. They had two other children, both girls, and the family lived in a brownstone on Manhattan's Upper West Side, summering at another home on Lake Canandaigua in upstate New York, where Bogart developed his passion for sailing. On the surface their life appeared close to the placid ideal of their time and place. And indeed, as he grew up, Humphrey Bogart had every reason to look forward to a comfortable and not overtaxing future. He was sent first to New York's select and socially impeccable Trinity School, later to the Phillips Academy in Andover, Massachusetts, then, as now, one of the nation's leading preparatory schools. Neither of them fully engaged his interest.

Life in the Bogart family was not, however, as serene and secure as it appeared on the surface. Belmont Bogart appears to have been a weak and charming man—very likely an alcoholic—not overly devoted to his work or his family's future; he was perfectly capable of setting aside his practice for months at a time in favor of hunting and fishing expeditions. Maud, in contrast, was a regal and reserved woman, about whom Bogart was later to say, "I can't say that I ever loved my mother. I admired her."

At Andover the boy began to stray from his preordained rut. He was expelled after three semesters for "incontrollable high spirits." Actually, according to Bogart, it was because he joined a group bent on ducking an unpopular teacher in a pond one night; he was the only member of the gang the victim recognized. The United States having entered World War I by that time, and Bogart loving boats and the water, joined the Navy. He served in a destroyer and as helmsman on a troop transport. It has been said that a wartime encounter with a flying wood splinter gave him the trademark scar on his upper lip, but that may not necessarily be so. On the whole, though, he had a good war; it was peace that came as a shock to him.

When he returned home, he discovered that his father had lost most of the family's money through careless investments. Even if Bogart had been interested in returning to formal education—Yale had been mentioned—there was now no possibility of that. Nor was there any possibility of idleness or a long search for a comfortable job. He had to find work immediately, doing whatever presented itself to him. He tried one or two avenues—including stockbrokerage, so often the salvation of indigent young men of good breeding—then caught on with William A. Brady, a famous producer, who had been a power in all aspects of show business since before the turn of the century, and who was married to the actress Grace

Here's Looking at You, Kid
Young Humphrey as a lively two-year-old,
togged out in dungarees he can grow into.

George. He had been a neighbor of the Bogarts, and his son, William Jr., had been one of Humphrey's best boyhood pals. The elder Brady took him on first as an office boy, then put him to work in his New York film production unit in several capacities, before appointing him company manager of one of his touring companies. Bogart took to kidding the lead in the show, Neil Hamilton, about the soft life that actors seemed to lead. On the tour's last night Hamilton fell ill and dared Bogart to go on in his place. He did—and froze. But later, when he was complaining to Brady about the lack of remuneration in backstage work, the producer casually replied, "Why don't you become an actor? Actors make good money."

And so he did. There was no conviction in the decision, certainly no grand passion. Nor did he appear to have an abounding natural gift. But it seemed to Brady and others who employed him that he was ideally suited to play juveniles of the class into which he had been born. He was not at first very good. Of his second Broadway appearance, in 1922's *Swifty*, Alexander Woollcott wrote: "The young man who embodies the sprig is what is usually and mercifully described as inadequate."

Still, he persevered, "a well-behaved, agreeable, serious young man," in the words of a colleague of those days. "I have politeness and manners. I was brought up that way," Bogart himself was to say many years later, and those qualities served him well, distracting audiences from his shortcomings in technique. And the fact that romantic comedy, of various degrees of sophistication, was a staple genre on Broadway in the 1920s helped, too. Not a year went by in which he did not have at least one role in one of these feathery concoctions. Legend has it that Bogart was the first to pipe the line that seemed to sum up, in two words, the entire vanished style that sustained him and perhaps the institution of the commercial theater in those days. It was "Tennis, anyone?"

It could be argued that during this phase of his career he was more appropriately cast, wearing blue blazer and flannels, uttering breezy inanities, than he was at any time by Hollywood in the subsequent decade. In any event, he acquired a bagful of actor's tricks, a patina of professionalism, and his first two wives, both actresses he had worked with (his marriage to Helen Menken lasted fewer than two years; that to Mary Philips for ten). But as the decade drew to a close, he was beginning to outgrow juvenile roles. The theater, too, was beginning to outgrow them, or anyway the kind of plays that required them.

Hollywood, however, was learning to talk. And it swept up actors, writers, and directors who were thought to have learned in their stage work how to handle the mysteries of dialogue. Bogart was carried along by this westward-streaming exodus. In 1930, the first year of the Depression, he signed a contract with Fox at four hundred dollars a week, under which he made five films, none of them significant for him or for the history of the medium. When his option was dropped, he returned to New York for one play, got more picture work in Hollywood, then, when it dried up, returned again to New York. "I wasn't Gable, and I flopped" was his brief latter-day comment.

By then he could afford to be offhand about his youthful follies. At the time he had reason

Anchors Aweigh
At attention, Seaman Bogart in 1918, after naval training at Pelham Park, emerging as coxwain.

to be anxious, and he apparently was. The Depression was entering its bleakest years, and his family's economic condition had worsened with the nation's. The work he was able to get in New York was all in short-lived shows. Around this time his father died in Bogart's arms, leaving him ten thousand dollars in debts to settle and a ruby and diamond ring his son was to wear for the rest of his life. Nor was that the end of the troubles in his house. One of his sisters died, also apparently the victim of drink, and his other sister fell prey to a chronic mental illness and was, as well, left penniless by a divorce, with a young child to care for. Bogart was her support, "emotionally and financially" (as Lauren Bacall put it), for the rest of her life.

Now, however, his professional luck began to change. He was cast in a play called *Invitation to a Murder*, in which he impressed producer Arthur Hopkins, who remembered him some months later when he was searching for someone to play the psychopathic Duke Mantee in *The Petrified Forest* on Broadway. Playwright Robert Sherwood, who was a friend of Bogart's, wanted him for another role in the piece, but Hopkins persisted, the star, Leslie Howard (after whom Bogart was to name his daughter) liked him, and all opened to approving reviews. In the course of the play's run Howard told Bogart he would do his best to see that he got a chance to repeat the role in the screen version, and he was as good as his word. Warner Brothers tested other actors and actually announced Edward G. Robinson for the role. When Bogart heard this, he cabled Howard, vacationing in Scotland, and Howard informed the studio that he would not play in the picture if Bogart was not cast in it.

So he got the part. And he made an impression in it, even though the movie is dreadful—all about Howard's fragile, wandering poet coming into deadly conflict with Bogart's psychopathic gangster in a café in the eponymous locale. Very high-toned and stagy—actually mummified—under Archie Mayo's all-too-respectful direction, it lacked the energy, conviction, and lunatic spirit of even the routine gangster movies of the time. But it did impress people for its fidelity to the play and the sobriety with which it took up what the audience was led to think of as large themes in a self-consciously literate manner. Within its static, claustrophobic context, Bogart's trapped-animal seething could not help commanding attention. It is perhaps too much to say you couldn't take your eyes off him, but certainly there was little else worth looking at.

If *The Petrified Forest* did not quite do for Bogart what *The Public Enemy* had done for Cagney or *Little Caesar* had done for Robinson, the studio could not help but notice the public noticing him. His roles in the next year and a half were many and mostly lengthy. Some of the programmers—*Bullets or Ballots*, *San Quentin*, *Marked Woman*—were solid melodramatic entertainments. And at least one of the pictures, *Black Legion*, released early in 1937, was better than that, a cautionary social comment aimed at the Ku Klux Klan and other secret organizations enforcing their racial and religious prejudices violently as hooded mobs.

Dead End, which Bogart made on loan-out to Goldwyn was, like *The Petrified Forest*, an

The Second Mrs. Bogart
Bogart with Mary Philips, who was with him on
Broadway in *Nerves* in 1924. They married in 1928.

adaptation of a Broadway hit, widely believed to be distinguished. It is, in its way, as stage-bound as the earlier piece, but it is not quite as draggy, if only because it ranges over wider emotional territory as it anatomizes New York slum life, personified by characters operating at various levels in it. Bogart's role is not large; he plays a criminal who returns home for a visit and discovers that his former lover has turned into a whore and that his mother despises him. The picture, of course, belongs to the Dead End Kids, a gang of streetwise boys who were to achieve ensemble stardom in a series of B movies that stressed the comic side of their rough good nature, though here they were touched by a measure of pathos as the principal victims of society's indifference. Be that as it may, Bogart's discovery of mutual alienation between himself and the society that formed him hints at larger and more poignant isolations to come for his screen character.

But from this point until 1940, for reasons not entirely clear, his career seemed to stall. The studio kept him busy, and he appeared in more than a few films with strong budgets and good casts. He was always in secondary roles, however, and clearly uncomfortable in them. He was notably edgy in the three films in which he worked with James Cagney—*Angels with Dirty Faces*, *The Oklahoma Kid*, and *The Roaring Twenties*. In them, Bogart's unredeemable badness was supposed to contrast with the vulnerable charm of Cagney's good-bad guys. But his hands always seemed too busy in these pictures, his eyes too shifty; in general, he was overplaying. Perhaps he was trying too hard to make an impression, but it seems likely that he simply could make no emotional connection with these supporting roles. He was bad in different ways in films like *The Amazing Dr. Clitterhouse*, in which he was supposed to play a more comical crook, and *Dark Victory*, in which, in his wildest miscasting, he was a broody stablehand, a sort of half-realized Laurentian figure, who was briefly the vaguely menacing lover of Bette Davis's neurotically high-strung heiress. In nothing he did at this time was he able to assert anything of his singularity. In nothing was he able to achieve dominance even in a single scene. In nothing was he able to impart something to the public that it could take home and dream upon. According to what seems a reliable accounting, he was hanged or electrocuted eight times, sentenced to life imprisonment nine times, and riddled by bullets a dozen times in his first forty-five movies. He was possibly in some danger of slipping down into that large, almost anonymous, stable of second leads and character men that Warner Brothers, like all the studios of the time, maintained to keep its production schedule rolling along as smoothly as possible.

Looking back on this period, one sees just how ludicrous the imputation of even unconscious existentialist qualities to Bogart is. It is a central tenet of existentialism, for example, that all of us must remake ourselves every day in order to face the day. And many philosophers of this school have found in the actor the figure that most clearly exemplifies this necessity. But Bogart's problem at this moment was precisely that he did not know how to remake himself— not persuasively, at any rate. In the meantime, nothing that came his way

Script Conference
Bogart and Leslie Howard run through a scene from
The Petrified Forest. Is Howard's pipe that noxious?

26 Bogie

"You're the last great apostle of rugged individualism."

Leslie Howard as Alan Squier in *The Petrified Forest*

offered him metaphors through which he could express some authentic aspect of himself.

One does not imagine that he could express his dilemma in those terms. But he was clearly aware that his personal life was at this time a misery. He and Mary Philips had drifted apart —she found her work mainly in New York—and their marriage came to an end in 1937. He married Mayo Methot, or "Sluggy," as he called her, in 1938, and almost immediately they began joint construction on the legend of "the battling Bogarts," as the press soon began styling them. Officially their rows were understood as affection displayed with a sort of perverse humor. And the public was encouraged to think of them as living a kind of black screwball comedy. But it requires no great leap of the imagination to read between the lines of the yellowing clippings and see that theirs was the story of two alcoholics locked in a punishing and dismal mutual dependency. Their screams at each other were, as we would now piously say, screams for help, which did not arrive for Bogart for six years and which never arrived for her.

Bogart, of course, never made any open complaint about her. To have done so would have been to violate his old-fashioned code of manners. Instead, his unhappiness leaked out in other ways. He was never a full-scale rebel against the exactions of the studio, as Cagney and Bette Davis were, but he was a constant complainer. "Bogie the beefer" is the way Raoul Walsh began thinking of him. He had directed Bogart in one of his early Fox films, and he was to be instrumental in his emergence as a star at Warner Brothers, but he remembered the actor grousing continually about the long hours moviemaking required in contrast with the stage. And about the early-morning calls. And about the bad food on location. And, of course, about the roles. Walsh always claimed that the only way to lure Bogart out of his blackness was to remind him of how good the money was in the movies as opposed to any other line of endeavor he might reasonably have undertaken.

And indeed, the money was more than a mere consolation to Bogart in these frustrating years. Toward his career he adopted an air of detached professionalism. "I'm known as a guy who always squawks about roles, but never refuses to play one," he told a reporter once. "I've never forgotten a piece of advice Holbrook Blinn gave me when I was a young squirt and asked him how I could get a reputation as an actor. He said, 'Just keep working.' The idea is that if you're always busy, sometime someone is going to get the idea that you must be good."

It is one of the oddities of Bogart's life that it is next to impossible to find in its record the slightest evidence that he ever reflected seriously on the art of acting. That was generally true of male movie stars of his era. For many of them acting was a rather suspect occupation, not quite an entirely suitable business for a real man to engage in, and one imagines Bogart seeing it that way. It perhaps overstates the case to say that he looked on it as no more than a job, like selling insurance or real estate, but it was surely something you did from nine to five (or longer in those hard-working studio days), then gratefully left behind as you drove home.

The way of life he established in Hollywood in these days, and clung to even after true

"Out of his blackness"
A pensive studio portrait from 1940. Soon he will make his breakthrough in *High Sierra* (1941).

stardom was accorded him, was a modest one. Aside from his public brawls with his third wife, Bogart attempted to live quietly. A lonely, literate and liberal-minded man, he was never a free spender, and his home on Horn Avenue in West Hollywood was comfortable, but by Hollywood standards unimpressive. His only indulgence was sailing, but in those days before he acquired his famous *Santana*, he owned only small boats, which he could handle alone, thereby gaining the silence and solitude he craved. When he was not working or sailing, he passed his days reading and working on chess problems; he had a reputation as an excellent amateur player.

But working or idle, when he was on land, he habitually ended his day at some fairly unpretentious restaurant since his taste was for booze and a certain unassuming, perhaps somewhat impersonal conviviality, not for great food or grand surroundings. Mike Romanoff's was a particular favorite. The host was a sort of living satire of Hollywood's social pretenses since he had styled himself a "prince," a descendant of the deposed Russian ruling family, and reveled in the fact that everyone knew his claim was fraudulent. Bogart's drinking companions rarely included actors or directors—Peter Lorre was an exception—and never executives. The majority of them were writers, but of a rather special type, which he had doubtless discovered in New York's speakeasy society of the 1920s. They generally had a foot in journalism but had drifted toward the more profitable lines of work—writing humor or popular fiction or plays. Now they were connected in various ways with the still-more profitable movies—some of them permanently, some of them only when their checking accounts needed a quick fix. His circle at various times included the likes of Mark Hellinger, Robert Benchley, John O'Hara, Lewis Bromfield, Nunnally Johnson, Quentin Reynolds, Dorothy Parker. Those directors who were permitted to join the circle—John Huston and Richard Brooks, for example—had some journalism in their resumes and were, indeed, *writer*-directors.

These people were funny and intelligent, but not self-revealing. As writers they despised literary pretension. As movie colonists they were *in* the business, but never quite *of* it in spirit. And many of them were quiet, mannerly, purposeful drinkers, uninterested in causing a disturbance unless they were themselves disturbed at their pastime by some loutish outsider. In this period it was typical of Bogart to find some of them on his way home from work and get an early start on the night's drinking. He would then continue on to his house, where he might rest a bit, change clothes, and possibly contemplate continuing his drinking in private. Sometimes he would. But more often, it seems, either marital discord or just inner restlessness would drive him back out into the night in search of his pals, from whom he did not part early. This pattern continued even after he had grown more successful and persisted in diminished degree even during his happy fourth marriage to Lauren Bacall. The difference was that he and she stayed home more and invited their friends to join them there for their quiet after-dinner revels. "I don't trust anyone who doesn't drink," Bogart often proclaimed, and there was more than bravado in that statement. It was a statement of principle, and he absorbed terrible physical punishment living up to it.

Called to the Bar
Said Nunnally Johnson: "Bogie had an alchoholic thermostat. He just set his thermostat at noon, pumped in some Scotch, and stayed at a nice even glow all day, automatically redosing if necessary."

If Bogart's lifestyle was essentially immutable, his career was, like all others in show business, amenable to a change in luck. In 1940 he finished the second of the pictures Raoul Walsh directed him in at Warner Brothers. It was *They Drive by Night*, a fairly gritty portrayal of freelance truckers fighting to keep their independence. In it he played a driver immobilized and embittered when he loses an arm in an accident. In the second half of the picture the plot spins entirely away from Bogart's character into a rather stylized murder melodrama primarily involving its lead, George Raft. But given a chance to play a victim, and rather a self-pitying one at that, Bogart was hard yet sympathetic in a way he had not been since the latter portion of *Black Legion*.

Now Walsh was set to do *High Sierra*, the adaptation of a novel by W. R. Burnett, one of the better, and still one of the least critically attended, of the hard-boiled crime writers (one of his novels formed the basis for *Little Caesar*), which Mark Hellinger was producing. From the start of his work on the script Huston had insisted that there was a spirit in Burnett that most previous film versions of his novels had not caught. Take out "the strange sense of inevitability that comes with our deepening understanding of his characters and the forces that motivate them," he wrote in a memo to production chief Hal Wallis, "and only the conventional husk of a story remains." He would successfully strive to keep that shadow of fatefulness in his script, and the result was for the most part austere and affecting, a sort of epitaph for the movies' gangster anti-heroes of the 1930s—still romantic, of course, but wearier and bleaker than, say, *Angels with Dirty Faces* or *The Roaring Twenties*, which both copped more sentimental pleas for Cagney as he expired.

Walsh was the ideal director for a project like this, a man who at his best trusted the subtexts to speak for themselves, while he banged the action along efficiently, unsentimentally, sometimes contrapuntally. And the central role of the ageing gangster growing vulnerable through the diminution of his formerly pure selfishness (he is undone by sentimental gestures toward a crippled girl and a winsome dog) was one any actor might have coveted—any actor, that is, but the ones the studio approached. Paul Muni turned it down because, he said, he didn't want to play another gangster, although he had only played one. According to Walsh, George Raft rejected it because he did not want to die in the end, although other accounts suggest Bogart slyly put the idea of the part's unsuitability into his rival's egocentric head. In any event, Bogart, who was friends with everyone significantly involved in creating the picture, actively campaigned for the part, and the studio finally gave it to him—though he was forced to take second billing to his costar, Ida Lupino, to whom he was so unpleasant during shooting that she refused to work with him again.

The seriousness with which he took the part of Roy Earle is signaled by his haircut. Up to the crown it is virtually shaved, strictly prison barbershop work, which is realistically correct for a man who has been behind bars for eight years, and very un-Hollywood. As is his psychology, for Roy Earle finds himself suddenly free in a world in which he begins to see —

The Mad Dog
In character for *High Sierra*, Bogart poses with carbine as renegade prison parolee Roy "Mad Dog" Earle.

as the result of a bungled robbery—that crime as he once practiced it is an anachronism, that he himself is an anachronism. That feeling was one Bogart knew something about. And the air of puzzled distaste for this new world was something the reluctant movie actor and citizen of Tinseltown could understand as well. There is about his Roy Earle the air of a man straining to pick out the melody in a new kind of music that grates harshly on his ears, an air, too, of a man who would just as soon die as try to adjust to a world that thinks this stuff is worth listening to. For the first time in a movie he gave a fully realized performance. And a touching one.

High Sierra was a hit. So was Bogart. Things moved so quickly at Warner Brothers that he had finished another quite forgettable picture before its success was clearly established. But when *The Wagons Roll at Night* was done, there was yet another picture and another Raft reject for him to help consolidate his new position. That was *The Maltese Falcon*, John Huston's adaptation of the Dashiell Hammett novel, which was also to be Huston's debut as a director. It is a film that depends more on the bold snap of its dialogue and the felicities of its casting than on showy directorial technique for its success. But at this stage of his career he was understandably more certain of his skills as a writer, and as a judge of writing (many of the script's best lines are taken directly from the book), than he was as a director. This was a point Howard Hawks always insisted he had made to Huston as he toiled for the shrewd older director on the script for *Sergeant York* and worried over what to select for his directorial debut. With sound basic material, Hawks said, all a director has to do is not screw up, as Huston definitely did not do.

The Maltese Falcon was also, and even more obviously, a wise choice for Bogart. It began the collaboration with Huston that would define, and continually refine, his stardom. More immediately it afforded him an opportunity to play another aspect of the radical self-sufficiency, and contempt for the conventional, that had distinguished his performance as Roy Earle. But with these differences: Where his hardness in *High Sierra* had about it a puzzled quality, here it gleamed brightly as he knifed through his scenes; where before his disgust with the world had rendered him nearly inarticulate, here it loosened his cynically quipping tongue; where before he had almost gratefully accepted his own death as atonement for his past sins, here he almost gratefully accepts the necessity of "sending over" the woman he says he loves to expiate her present sins. Sam Spade is not the sort of man who ought to have any woman in his life permanently—we understand that. In his fine character sketch of Bogart, Alistair Cooke, who knew him at the end of his life, speaks of the puritan streak in the man. He also drew an interesting analogy between the modern private eye and his progenitor Sherlock Holmes, pointing out that they shared two important traits: A fondness for arcane knowledge and a tendency toward depression, which may account for their bachelor status.

In *The Maltese Falcon* it is, finally, Sam Spade's moral firmness that provides the

Stuff Dreams are Made Of
Bogart (Sam Spade), shares the frame with the black bird,
cause of trouble in John Huston's *The Maltese Falcon* (1941).

mainspring of the story. In the end he has to establish the fact that though he may condone certain violations of the legal code as acceptably human frailties (thus encouraging the unobservant to miss his fundamental commitment to a larger morality), there are certain violations of his professional code (letting the murderer of his partner go free) and his personal code (pathological lying by someone who claims to love him and probably does after her fashion) that he cannot let anyone get away with.

This, too, was something Bogart could understand, for it was an aspect of his own character, the motive for the sudden, if occasional, irate outbursts he let slip from behind his habitual mask of aloofness and indifference. This recognition seemed to energize Bogart. For the first time he was truly hypnotizing, and unambiguously attractive, on the screen, and the best critic of the day, Otis Ferguson, recognized it immediately: "He has a good part here, a steady outlet for that authority and decision and hard level talk of his ... he fills it *without trying* and you're with him." Without trying. Yes. At last. And the public now had what it required of all movie stars in those days—a reliable sense of a screen character, a feeling that they knew what they were bargaining for when they paid their money to see one of his pictures. And from this point onward, with his name fixed firmly above the title, he became what a star has to be—a genre unto himself.

There was other, more routine business to conduct before finding his apotheosis in *Casablanca*. This included one more George Raft reject (would Bogart have become Bogart if Raft had not been so determinedly Raft, a crude and dim-witted egomaniac?). It was *All Through the Night*, about a Runyonesque group of mobsters called upon to unmask a Nazi spy ring in New York. Bogart was never comfortable in comedy and never comfortable attempting a lower-class accent. But the picture was amiable in its little way, and it did prefigure the main lines of his wartime work, in which he often played a man required to set aside his personal interests in order to serve the cause. He followed that with his last gangster film for Warner's, *The Big Shot*, and then teamed with Huston again for what we would nowadays call a spin-off, a picture that reassembled much of the cast of *Falcon* and attempted to re-create its mood.

The somewhat hasty air of *Across the Pacific* doubtless reflects the fact that war having broken out, Huston was awaiting the call to take up his commission in the U.S. Army Signal Corps, for which he made three extraordinary documentaries—the best any of the Hollywood contingent made for the government during the hostilities. There is a myth that Huston left Bogart in a pretty pickle—imprisoned by Japanese spies intent on blowing up the Panama Canal with no obvious way out—leaving Vincent Sherman, who finished the picture, to somehow get the star out of his predicament. But that seems not to have been so. Huston and Sherman spent a few days together, working out details and the picture concludes on a note of graceful improbability that has ever been a Hollywood specialty. We may note, for what it's worth, that *Across the Pacific* was the first, but not the last, film in which Bogart played a man declassed. He was an army officer who agreed to undergo a false court-martial and allow

himself to be cashiered from the service in order to make him a plausible target for Japanese espionage agents to recruit. But no—or small—matter. It was time, at last, for apotheosis.

A certain amount of myth attends the making of *Casablanca*, as it nearly always does the creation of legendary films. Mainly these stories revolve around the notion that it was meant to be a routine program feature, not a major effort on the part of Warner Bros. This idea derives, in turn, from a trial balloon press release indicating that it would star Anne Sheridan, Ronald Reagan and Dennis Morgan, the male stars in particular having been largely employed in Warner Bros. B pictures at the time. But as A. M. Sperber and Eric Lax prove in their long, definitive biography of Bogart, that is not so.

As everyone knows, the film was based on an unproduced play, *Everyone Comes to Rick's*, written by Murray Burnett and Joan Alison, but based on authentic experiences of the former. He and his wife had been touring Europe in 1937 and found themselves in Vienna at the time of the *anschluss*. There they had observed the arrogant triumphalism of the occupying Nazis, the vicious anti-Semitism of the populace, and found themselves carrying valuables out of the country for their Jewish-Austrian friends. A little later, in the south of France, they were struck by the indifference to the gathering storm that they found there. They even visited a nightclub where a black piano player was featured and Burnett found himself thinking the place would be a great setting for a play.

The work he wrote with Alison on his return featured almost all the basic beats of the finished movie: The romantically damaged Rick, an anti-Nazi and his wife trying to escape German hegemony, the letters of transit that are the fulcrum of the plot, even a merrily cynical French police chief. And, yes, there is a scene where the anti-Nazi encourages the singing of the *Marseillaise* by the nighclub's patrons. The big difference between play and film is that the anti-Nazi is transformed from a Czech munitions maker into an authentic resistance leader and that his wife, though still carrying a torch for Rick, is changed from an American "adventuress" into an upper-class European woman, which is why Ann Sheridan was replaced eventually by Ingrid Bergman.

This play was rescued from the slush pile in Warner's New York office by Irene Lee, the studio's West Coast story editor, while she was there on a visit. She had a good track record with acquisitions and better still had the ear of Hal Wallis, who had been for many years in charge of production at Warner Bros. and was now beginning a new contract as an independent producer with the studio. The piece suited his taste, which was for dark romantic dramas. Others were less confident about the play—some thinking it was pretty much tosh, especially in comparison with Lillian Hellman's *Watch on the Rhine*, which was, at the moment, the studio's major ant-fascist project.

Still, writers were assigned—lots of them. There were the Epstein brothers, Julius and Philip, specialists in adaptation and merry thorns in Jack Warner's side (they tended to get their day's work done in a couple of hours, which flew in the face of his stern belief that

"I Stick My Neck Out for No One"
His most famous role, Rick in *Casablanca*
(1942), which created a great romantic hero.

40   Bogie

writers should sit stoically at their typewriters from nine to five, since he was paying for a full day's work). There was Howard Koch, formerly of Orson Welles's Mercury Theatre, where he had written the infamous radio adaptation of *The War of the Worlds*, who was brought in to punch up the political themes (he was something of a Stalinist in those days, and soon to be the author of the propagandistic *Mission to Moscow*). There was Casey Robinson, whose strong suit was women's pictures, with an emphasis on romances going awry. They all hammered away at the thing, seeing it generally as a variation on *Algiers*, especially, perhaps, in its nostalgia for Paris, the relationship between hero and policeman, the ambiguities of its central romantic core. It was sold to David O. Selznick, when he was approached to loan out Ingrid Bergman to the film. "It's going to be a lot of shit like *Algiers*," one of the Epsteins said to him in the course of their successful pitch for her services.

The major problem presented by *Casablanca* (Hal Wallis retitled the piece, shamelessly echoing *Algiers*) was its ending. Hollywood never likes romantic renunciations; it believes the public requires hero and heroine to walk into the sunset hand in hand. Yet the logic of this story was implacably the opposite. So everyone dithered over it, virtually until the day it had to be shot. Ingrid Bergman once told me that she had been instructed to play the scene where Bogart rejects her "in the middle," with its full implications to be perhaps supplied in a coda. She didn't like that; what actress would? But Julius Epstein identified the moment when it all became clear to him and his brother. They were on the way to the studio, but stopped at the long light at the corner of Beverly Glen and Sunset, when one or the other of them, in effect, said "screw it," they have to separate.

Whatever, one is tempted to say. Sometimes what must be, must be. And besides, at this point in the war, with the issue still very much in doubt, Americans were ready for renunciations, for idealistic and inspirational sacrifices. And they needed—wanted—to see handsome, glamorous, people making them. It is, in the context of its moment, the only possible ending—and not entirely an unhappy one.

Narrative logic—or should one say emotional logic—is essential to any movie that attaches itself permanently to our memories and sensibilities and, structurally, especially after the problem of its ending was solved, *Casablanca* satisfies that need. But that's only part of the reason it goes on working so well. The wit and rue of its dialogue—the "I came to Casablanca for the waters" exchange is one example, but so is "Round up the usual suspects" and the observation that when the Germans marched into Paris they were wearing grey while Ilsa was in blue. It doesn't take a lot of writing like that to establish a movie's tone, but there is more than enough of it in *Casablanca* to grant it a powerfully pleasurable hold on us. In later years Howard Koch took to attending screenings of the picture at various colleges and he reported the students chorusing the famous lines as they occurred, as if they were at, say, one of the ritualistic showings of *The Rocky Horror Picture Show*. In those days there was an emphasis on well-crafted dialogue in American movies—probably a result of the many witty, literate

"We'll Always Have Paris"
Bogart and his Swedish co-star Ingrid Bergman break
open the champagne.

playwrights and novelists who came to Hollywood in the first decades of sound production—
that began to disappear a decade or so later.

There's also the matter of direction to consider. Michael Curtiz, with his ability to handle
almost any subject (in this same year he also directed *Yankee Doodle Dandy*) has never been
regarded as a true auteur; he made too many films on too many wildly disparate topics. But
this film—with its shadowy lighting and its opportunities for the tracking shots he loved, not
to mention the air of *weltschmerz* that hung over it, was perfectly attuned to his middle-
European spirit. He may not have been the picture's auteur, but he served it impeccably.

But perhaps its greatest good fortune lay in the area where luck is the most important
factor in production, which is casting. Bogart aside, almost every other significant role in the
picture nearly went to someone else. Hedy Lamarr, not Ingrid Bergman, was the first choice
for Ilsa. Paul Henried, so noble, clueless and touching as Victor Lazlo, was tied up on another
picture. People thought a French actor would have been better as the police captain than the
very English Claude Rains. Wallis, for some reason, was hesitant about using Dooley Wilson
as the pianist (in part, possibly, because Wilson could not actually play the piano). Add in the
reliably comic menaces, Peter Lorre and Sidney Greenstreet, and this cast signals that all
thoughts of this being just a routine release had disappeared.

What no one could imagine, until they saw the dailies, was just how perfect they were all
going to be in their roles. This is particularly true of Bergman and Bogart. The former had, of
course, been imported from Sweden by David Selznick, mainly to star in an American remake
of *Intermezzo*, in which she had been a hit in her native land and elsewhere. The publicity
about her at the time emphasized the "freshness" of her beauty, the lack of makeup with which,
it was said, she always faced the cameras. She was supposed to represent a kind of innocence,
thus something of a reversal on the *femme fatales* Hollywood typically imported from Europe.
This was far from the case. She was a free-spirited, sexually restless woman, whose true nature
belied the saints and nuns she took to playing a few years later and which, when her affair with
Roberto Rossellini became publicly known, brought her to scandalous infamy.

She is radiantly beautiful in *Casablanca*, but more important the film represents an early
example of her playing romance "in a mood of torment, indecision and incipient suffering" to
borrow a nice phrase from David Thomson. She respects her heroic husband, knows how
much he needs her, but cannot deny the heat Rick Blaine awakens in her. We are speaking
here of sexuality's eternal mystery—the fact that some people just wantonly turn us on, while
others awaken in us only dutifulness. Bergman obviously knew something about that, and the
way she conveys the itchy passion boiling beneath her respectable mask—especially
considering the constraints imposed on such performances by the motion-picture production
code at the time—has an authenticity about it that keeps breaking through the film's
conventional romantic bonds.

The same, only more so, can be said of Bogart, because he is easeful here, instinctively at

home with his character, in a way he had not been before. That kind of comfort, that blending of a factual self with a fictional creation, in which neither the performer nor the audience is entirely aware of where the one ends and the other begins, is rare. But it is a basic requirement for screen actors working at the star level and hoping to stay there for a while. Think about it: He is playing the proprietor of a "gin joint" of the sort he had been habituating most of his adult life; more significantly, he is a man mourning not just a lost love but the lost idealism of his youth, the better man he might have been if things had worked out differently for him.

We don't know a lot about Rick—only that he was involved in some sort of disreputable, but not necessarily dishonorable, activities in the United States when he was younger (left-wing politics perhaps?) and that he ran guns to the right sides (that is, the left sides) in Spain and Ethiopia prior to the outbreak of World War II in Europe. These were, of course, lost causes, and we are allowed to imagine—though the movie never says as much—that there was something redemptive about his affair with Ilsa in Paris, the sudden failure of which drove him finally to that state of bitterness and dark depression ("I stick my neck out for nobody") in which we discover him in *Casablanca*.

There are two elements in the dilemmas Rick confronts that, I think, struck a chord with the generation that rediscovered Bogart in the sixties, each of which any more or less sensitive individual standing on the brink of adulthood must confront for the first, but not the last, time in life. One is the attempt to weigh personal desire—his need to reclaim his lost love—against the moral imperatives placed demandingly before him by urgent political and social forces—her putative value to the cause of worldwide anti-fascism—and strike the correct balance between them. If you look at this issue objectively, when you are not in thrall to *Casablanca*'s slick persuasiveness, it is a false one. One really thinks that Victor Lazlo, true believer that he is, could get along without Ilsa. Sure he'd miss her, and remain permanently pissed off with her for staying behind with Rick, but he's a busy and important guy, with plenty of world-historical matters to preoccupy him. I don't think he'd be thrown that far off course by her defection. But what has reality to do with high, sacrificial romance? With love well lost for glittering ideology, why save yourself when, with a little more effort, you can save the world? It is ever an attractive idea, especially to the kind of youthful idealists who embraced the Bogartian ethos some twenty years later.

There is also the closely related matter of nostalgia to consider. Rick's time with Ilsa in Paris was clearly the most intense passage of his life, implicitly more riveting than any of his old, politically motivated adventures. He cannot put those months behind him. To do so would be to abandon his best self. (It is only when he discharges those memories with his final renunciation of Ilsa that he can transcend the dark stasis that has overcome him in Casablanca, then retreat, as it were, back to the future). As any parent has reason to observe (and remember), the late-adolescent discovery that childhood, that mixed bag of irresponsible pleasure and protective custody, is forever lost comes as an unpleasant shock. There is a tendency among young adults to indulge in instant nostalgia for it—to mourn in a Salingeresque manner for their recently lost innocence. There is, I'm convinced, an analogy between this mood and Rick's inability to abandon his feelings for the purity of his lost love.

When *Casablanca* was being written and shot did anyone realize what potent messages were being encoded in it? Of course not! The amount of merry cynicism about the project that one finds in the memos and memories surrounding its creation is astonishing and in some sense heartening. Nobody took the damn thing seriously—except possibly as a promising commercial proposition. In his acute essay on the movie Umberto Eco makes the point that its success depends on the fact that it is an almost perfect compendium of the conventions (or clichés) of the adventure-romance film as they had developed to date. He claims there is not a single one of them that the picture fails to evoke, with the result that its manic generosity—in the snap of its dialogue, in the richness of cinematographer Arthur Edeson's imagery, in the controlled lushness of Max Steiner's score—simply overwhelms disbelief. It is one of those rare cases where less would have been ... less.

Except in the case of Humphrey Bogart, where less really was more. When the picture went into release and became an instant success, the press quickly jumped on the fact that he was an unlikely figure of romance. He was a compact man (five feet, nine inches tall, weighing in at 155 pounds) who turned forty-four the month the picture opened, balding and rather obviously showing the wear and tear of his hard-lived life. He was, moreover, as compact emotionally as he was in stature. He did not permit his feelings, in this film or any other, to slosh about and spill over in ways that elicit instant sympathy. Raymond Chandler, who knew something about hard, emotionally hidden men, wrote of Bogart a little later, that he could be "tough without a gun, Also, he has a sense of humor that contains that grating undertone of contempt." Comparing Bogart to other movie hardcases he saw in him a mature and well-earned flintiness that the likes of, say, Alan Ladd, just could not touch. Bogart, he thought, was "the genuine article."

But tough guys who are merely tough, quickly grow tiresome, as Bogart's earlier career had taught him. Now in early middle age, he was bringing something else to the party. There is something appraising in his eyes, a weariness and a wariness that grounds a movie always in danger of flightiness and unconscious risibility, in a recognizable reality. This is a movie in which everyone—Bogart included—has a sad story or a hidden agenda, and he's the guy who has to sort out what is true and what is untrue among all the fictions and factions contending for his attention. The reserve he brings to this task, the sense he conveys of having seen it all and heard it all, is truly very seductive.

For wartime movies had the unfortunate effect of turning their heroes into blabbermouths. That fascism could not be permitted sway in the world no decent person doubted. That defeating this noxious ideology was an urgent necessity was painfully obvious. But action

movies (westerns, crime dramas, accounts of heroism in historical warfare) had not previously required their heroes to explain themselves at length. Whatever evil they were opposing was self-evidently ugly. So it should have been, one thinks, in World War II. But there was a need in America, especially early in the war, with its former isolationism still fresh in everyone's mind, to enlist everyone—no slackers allowed—in the great struggle. Thus nearly every war movie contained a character, not unlike Rick Blaine, who had to be lured out of his selfishness, mobilized for a rather abstract righteousness. This led to a second very common trope in these films, which was the noble speech spoken either as an epitaph over those who had made the supreme wartime sacrifice or as the hero prepared himself (and the audience) for his own untimely extinction. Quite often in these moments they spoke lengthily about the better postwar world they were helping to purchase with their deaths. Implicit in these speeches was the curious (and utterly unproven) belief that ordinary citizens would calmly accept death in order to advance abstract, if uplifting, ideals. These films, in effect, offered cheap ideological answers to the enigma of heroism. That the men who actually placed themselves in harm's way in combat never thought or spoke in these ways, that they fought largely to survive—or at best for the men in their units fighting beside them—was not a thought Hollywood permitted itself to entertain until very late in the war, and then only rarely (see *They Were Expendable* or *The Story of G.I. Joe* and very little else).

So, taking nothing away from his performance, Bogart was lucky. He was lucky to be in an early wartime film before the sentiments he finally expressed in its closing moments became clichés. And he was lucky to be in a film in which the horrors of mass killing were never shown, not even alluded to. Basically, *Casablanca* is an insouciant and optimisitic film, full of the kind of quips and barbs and comic types that had, until recently, made romantic comedy such a delightful American genre. And that, too, was a lucky thing. For it was in production during truly desperate days, right after the United States had been thrust into World War II unprepared, when, frankly, the war's outcome, despite all the brave home-front propaganda, was very much in doubt. Even though the tide seemed at least slightly to be turning by the time it was released, we very much needed a movie in its vein—something smart and amusing and reasonably suspenseful that reminded us of the movies's best pre-war spirit. Also remember that no one except the hateful Major Strasser gets dead in the film. Such sacrifices as it calls on its principals to make really don't amount to much more than "a hill of beans" as Bogart finally puts it. We emerge from the film inspired and misty eyed and thinking that if Rick and Ilsa could make the romantic sacrifice they did, we might be able to do the same.

The film's ability to keep the real war off-screen has, of course, served it well over the years. It renders war's ghastly essence abstract, distant, therefore bearable. If that's all there is to it—a kiss in the shadows while the perfectly timed cough of an airplane's engine signals an end to the fun and games—why, as one might say, "bring it on." Or so subsequent generations, looking for bravery without bloodshed, were led to believe. That the picture went

The Day the Wehrmacht Reached Paris
Rick later recalled: 'I remember every detail.
The Germans wore gray, you wore blue.'

into release within days of the announcement that Casablanca had been the site of an actual conference between Roosevelt and Churchill (it was on this occasion that they announced the dubious policy of insisting on the "unconditional surrender" of the Axis) was a further blessing to the film—millions of dollars worth of free publicity.

Casablanca sealed Bogart's stardom. About that there is no question and no dispute. Yet, once again, he said very little about it. He brought solid professionalism to his work on the picture, often beginning the work day by arguing with the director, the writers, the producer about this or that aspect of the way the story was developing (generally in great haste). This was generally a ruse; he often needed time to memorize the lines he had not studied the night before. He apparently enjoyed his work with Bergman in a non-committal sort of way, though he was heard to say that he thought it preposterous for any man to give up a woman as beautiful as she was, no matter how noble the reasons for so doing. Mayo Methot, her marriage to Bogart definitely on the wane, thought perhaps he might have had a brief fling with Bergman, but no one else did. In the months after it was released he let it be known that he had not yet seen the finished film, implying that Methot, her jealousy still raging, forbade it. Later on, he neither crowed nor glowed about the film; it was just something he had done that had turned out all right.

I suspect age had something to do with this temperateness. In his day, stardom was not always thrust prematurely on actors and actresses. Most of them served fairly long apprenticeships on the stage before the movies found them, and since the audience for films was not in those days dominated, as it now is, by adolescents and post-adolescents, that was okay with the public. And, I think, good for the stars. Like Bogart, many of them had been up and down for years and so knew something about fame's fickleness. Their heads were not always swelled by success nor were their spirits necessarily shrivelled by failure. We may pause, slightly puzzled, over the unlikely posthumous adoration accorded a middle-aged actor by the sixties generation, but one also thinks Bogart might have shrugged it off. Stranger things had happened to him in life.

There was quite a long wait between *Casablanca*'s opening and the prizes it collected at the Academy Awards—over a year—and Bogart filled the interim with routine work. He played a merchant marine first officer who had risen from deckhand in *Action in the North Atlantic*, and a professional soldier, a sergeant commanding a tank separated from its unit, in *Sahara*. Both were working-class figures and in the former he very nicely underplayed his big scene, in which he was required to conduct a burial at sea of a group of sailors, killed in a raid, who represented every major American race, creed, and ethnic group. In the latter he had to hold together a smaller, but similarly mixed, crew (and assorted wayfarers they picked up) under assault from a Nazi horde and the desert climate. Here more Popular Front rhetoric was required of him (John Howard Lawson, truest of the true Communist believers among the Hollywood Ten, wrote both these films), but Bogart knew how to throw that stuff away, make

Free-wheeling
Bogart used a bicycle to get around the Warner-Burbank lot. He once drunkenly cycled around shouting, "Look, no hands!" until Jack Warner came out to admonish him.

it sound almost naturalistic. And in both pictures he was spared—or perhaps insisted on sparing himself—from carrying the heaviest message.

Passage to Marseilles, released in 1944 is an altogether more interesting film than either of its immediate predecessors, though it is more obviously a failure because of its inability to realize its complex ambitions. You can tell its story quite simply: Bogart plays a character named Marac, formerly a French newspaper publisher, whose pre-war warnings against Germany and its French sympathizers have landed in him jail on a trumped-up murder charge. And not just any jail: He is incarcerated in the notorious French hell hole on Devil's Island. He and some companions make a daring escape, are picked up by a French steamer, fight off a Nazi sympathizer on board as well as a strafing Luftwaffe plane. He then makes his way to England, where he joins a Free French bomber squadron. Sometimes, on its way home from its runs over Europe it flies over a farmhouse where his wife (a luminous Michele Morgan) and child have taken refuge. He drops them loving messages via parachute. He is, however, killed on one of his missions and Claude Rains reads out his last, inspirational message to his son, which is as endless as his statement of principle in *Casblanca* was brief, then orders one of the planes to deliver it to the boy. I said the story was fairly simple. But the screenwriters, Casey Robinson and Jack Moffitt chose to tell it through a series of flashbacks—often enough flashbacks borne of yet other flashbacks—that needlessly complicate the story and the picture (which was obviously intended to reinvoke the *Casablanca* spirit—same director and some of the same actors) more or less collapsed from structural strain. But it does have a nice noirish look to it and one must say that it represents the longest fall through the class structure—from dapper prosperity to rags, starvation and sadism on Devil's Island—that Bogart was ever obliged to endure in a movie. It makes his character, discovered in his final aviator incarnation, uncommonly sullen and uncommunicative. We understand that he has, literally, suffered more than words can say.

There is one other element in the film that is worth mentioning. In the sequence where the German airplane is shot down, some members of its crew are rescued by the crew of the steamer. Whereupon Bogart's character simply murders them in cold blood. He screams justification for his action, but it is a truly shocking scene, without parallel in any American war movie before or since. It was always important to show Allied forces fighting fairly, honorably in movies. It was for the Japanese and the Germans to commit mindless atrocities. We can perhaps understand Marac to be temporarily unhinged by his brutal experiences, but the sequence was so shocking that, after the war, the film was banned in England and it remains discomfiting to this day, when killing in the movies is much more casual than it was in the 1940s.

It was the sort of thing one might have expected Bogart to argue against, given his growing image as a growly proponent of liberal-minded civility. Perhaps he was distracted; he was in the midst of a vicious argument with Jack Warner over another picture (*Conflict*), with the

Middle-aged Stardom
Bogart, in his mid-forties, now an unassailable star,
after nearly twenty-five years as an actor.

mogul insisting he play the ungrateful role of a wife-murderer and threatening to give his *Marseille* role to Jean Gabin. It was also becoming clear to him that his marriage to Methot had reached the hopeless stage, which upset him more than one might have imagined.

That problem, at least, was approaching a solution, though he could not see it at the time. The instrument of his deliverance was slippery, scheming, self-aggrandizing Howard Hawks, who just happened to be a great charmer and, just possibly, the greatest of American directors. As usual, he was in trouble at the time—mired in gambling debts and obliged to surrender half of his Warner Bros. salary to the IRS to cover unpaid taxes. Nevertheless, he had in his possession the rights to Ernest Hemingway's novel, *To Have and Have Not*, which he had acquired earlier, when Hemingway had needed money, lost but then reacquired. Hawks always argued that it was his friend's "worst" book, but said he could make a good movie out of—mostly, as it turned out, by excising almost everything in it but its basic situation.

Hawks also had under personal contract a nineteen-year-old New York model named Betty Perske, soon to be rechristened Lauren Bacall. It was his wife of the time who noticed her picture in a fashion magazine and urged her upon him. His faithful screenwriting collaborator, Jules Furthman, had done a passable adaptation of the book and Hawks's other great friend, William Faulkner, began doing what he did best, restructuring Furthman's work and, most important, spinning the story away from tragedy and toward a more contemporary angle. Harry Morgan, the central figure, now became a reluctant enlistee in the war against fascism, when the villains were changed, by Faulkner, into Nazi-sympathizing Frenchmen operating out of Martinique. It was sort of *Casablanca*, but with a brighter, harder, funnier edge.

That's not why we continue to attend *To Have and Have Not*. We go to it for the humorous heat of the romance between Bogart and Bacall, which developed on the set and was reflected in their playing. The director had detected in the off-screen Bogart a quality he had not yet brought to the screen. He called it "insolence," and he wanted to feature that quality in this picture. As Hawks later told the story, his largest effort so far as Bogart was concerned was getting him to smile; the actor had always felt that his scarred lip made him look grotesque when he tried to put on a happy face. This was the sort of small, sly manipulation in which Hawks specialized. He liked to unsettle actors by forcing them out of their tested mannerisms; it enlivened their performances, naturally, but it also rendered them insecure and thus more amenable to his powerful will.

There was no problem in making Bacall insecure. Totally inexperienced as an actress, perhaps a little overawed by the company she suddenly found herself in, her preparation for the picture consisted largely of reading passages from *The Robe* loudly, in her deepest voice, while sitting in a parked car near Mulholland Drive. Hawks wanted to develop a slightly masculine quality in her and thought vocal quality was key to achieving that. In Hawks's word, he was "inventing" her, turning her into what she became, *par excellence*, the so-called

Sultry Newcomer
Lauren Bacall made her electric debut with Bogart, her self-confidence and beauty concealing a lack of acting experience.

Hawksian woman—that is to say, a woman who is knowingly humorous in her dealings with men, tolerant of their foibles, always willing to go along uncomplainingly on their foolish adventures, and, above all, direct and uncomplicated in her sexual exchanges with them.

It worked. She may have been young, but she was tougher than her willowy, slightly boyish looks seemed to promise; there was something about her that no one had ever seen before on a screen, certainly nothing that Bogart had ever played opposite, and long before she captured the public's attention, she captured Bogart's, somewhat to Hawks's dismay. (He may have been jealous; he may merely have been concerned about his investment in her.) But taught to smile by the director and taught to love by Bacall, he responded with the most unshadowed performance of his career. His cynicism here was all on the surface, a manner of speaking as it were, not the sign of some deep disappointment. And in his scenes with Bacall there was an unguarded quality, a pleasurableness he had never demonstrated before in his screen dealings with women. Some years later John Huston asked a group of dinner guests if there was a period of their lives they would live over if they could. Most of them shrugged noncommittally, but Bogart replied, "Yes, when I was courting Betty." Hawks's comment, also made many years later was: "Bogie fell in love with the character she played, so she had to keep playing it the rest of her life." There is a certain shrewdness in that remark, if not, perhaps, the whole story.

For there was more pain in that courtship than he chose to let on. In her autobiography Bacall recounts an affair that seemed to consist largely of soulful hand-holding in parked cars on the way home from work, hours snatched here or there in inconvenient circumstances, and many an after-midnight phone call from Bogart, as he wandered nighttown, drinking his conflict into temporary remission. For though he had clearly come to loathe the farce he had been playing with Methot, he was aware that her drinking had reduced her to a pathetic state, and now she was promising to make one last attempt to cure her addiction. A decent man could not leave her at such a moment, and, Bacall implies he implied, should she recover, he would not have a valid excuse to leave her. It was not something a gentleman of the old school would do.

But, of course, he eventually did, in part perhaps because *To Have and Have Not* was a major hit. Even before the public endorsed it, the studio was pressing Hawks to come up with a new pairing of Bogart and Bacall, which threw them inescapably back together again professionally. This, of course, was *The Big Sleep*. The picture was in production during what was perhaps the worst period in Bogart's romance with Bacall, as he thrashed back and forth between her and his wife. But *The Big Sleep* went well, eliciting from Jack Warner a famous memo: "Word has reached me that you are having fun on the set. This must stop." Somehow, however, the first cut of the picture did not reflect the spirit in which the film was made. According to Todd McCarthy's punctilious biography of Hawks, this was much more narratively coherent than the final release version, but was rather dull. Philip Epstein was called in to supply the missing brightness, and this he did—most notably the exchange

"You Know How to Whistle"
The first film together was Howard Hawks' version of
Ernest Hemingway's *To Have and Have Not* (1944).

Following Pages **Hollywood's Favorite Couple**
By *The Big Sleep* (1946) Bogart had found a new wife,
a case of fourth time lucky, with Lauren Bacall as his ideal.

between Bogart and Bacall, in which horse-racing language becomes a metaphor for sexual teasing. To this day one wonders how that scene slipped past the censors; it could not be more blatant. But these late fixes—talk about insolence!—made the picture a hit when it was released in 1946.

By which time Bogart and Bacall were happily married. They accepted each other as they were. He did not attempt to remake her according to some womanly ideal of his own—always a temptation when a man is a quarter of a century older than his wife. She did not object when he had to howl at the moon with his pals. But more and more they were quietly at home together, often in the company of other couples. He still drank prodigiously, but, it seems, with much less desperation.

Most of his work for the next couple of years, was, however, rather routine. He was once again radically declassed in *Dead Reckoning*, where he is a decorated war hero investigating the disappearance of his best wartime buddy. Before he solves the case, he is himself accused of murder and reduced to fugitive status and into a love affair with a near-psychopathic female. In *Dark Passage* he reteamed with Bacall as a formerly well-to-do citizen, escaping from false imprisonment for the murder of his wife and seeking her real killers. He is on the run for the length of the movie, has to resort to plastic surgery and Bacall's kindness as a woman he encounters by chance in order to stay a half step ahead of his many pursuers.

It does seem, though, that the newfound sense of calmness and security Bogart found in his marriage seemed to have a freeing effect on him as an actor. He began to take risks that many performers at his age and station in life cannot make themselves try. John Huston was obviously a major force in pushing him in new directions, one of which was paranoia. This was not a vein American movies may be said to have explored very often previously. And never before as unblinkingly, and with such scarifying wit, as Bogart brought to his portrayal of Fred C. Dobbs in 1947's *The Treasure of the Sierra Madre*. Walter Huston cackled an Oscar-winning counterpoint of sanity as he led greenhorn miners Bogart and Tim Holt to their El Dorado in the Mexican mountains, but he was, in the end, powerless to stop Bogart's character from cracking under the weight of sudden wealth. That, too, was a masterstroke of casting by his son, who won writing and directing Academy Awards for the picture. The elder Huston had been a worthy presence in the movies for years, a fine actor too often forced to stand on his dignity. No one was prepared for his toothless, jigging, goatish energy in this film. But no one was prepared for Bogart's performance either—braggadocio alternating with sniveling, with both emerging out of a steady mutter of demented suspicions and wild schemings. It is very bold work, acting that is clearly based on observation and imagination rather than on attractively polished aspects of his private self. And it is brave work, never once pausing to cop a sympathetic plea.

The picture went wildly over budget and schedule and didn't make money, though it won a

For Keeps
The cake-cutting at the wedding, May 21, 1945,
not in California but at Louis Bromfield's farm in Ohio.

60   Bogie

new regard for Bogart in critical circles. All that, however, was in the future and was overshadowed by a political storm that, according to his friends, cost Bogart dearly.

As work on *Treasure* drew to a close, the House Committee on UnAmerican Activities began its notorious hearings on Communist influence on the motion-picture industry. It was never much and it was mostly ludicrous (though it must be said that the Hollywood Stalinists took themselves with a desperate seriousness). In any event, after preliminary hearings in Los Angeles, a full-scale inquiry was scheduled for Washington in October 1947. A group of prominent movie liberals, styling themselves the Committee for the First Amendment, decided to charter a plane to the capital where they would offer their support to the beleaguered Communists. The likes of John Huston, William Wyler, and screenwriter Philip Dunne were among the committee's prominent organizers and they recruited a number of major stars for the jaunt to Washington, among them Danny Kaye, Gene Kelly, June Havoc and Betty and Humphrey Bogart. The latter had been chastised earlier for his very public support of Franklin D. Roosevelt during his campaign for a fourth term, but he had defended himself strongly. In effect, he said that he had the same right as any American to his opinions and did not see why movie stardom should prevent him from speaking his piece.

But this was different. The CFA was composed of traditional liberals. Many of them did not believe that the nineteen Hollywood figures subpoenaed by HUAC were, indeed, Communist Party members; they thought they were just slightly more radicalized versions of themselves. Others didn't care whether they were or were not CP members; they felt they had a right to their opinions. None saw in the profession of communist beliefs any great threat to the republic, in which opinion they were correct. But as they often did when confronting government the communists insisted on taking an intransigent stance. They would challenge the committee's right to inquire into their beliefs and affiliations. Initially they took the position that they would be happy to speak to that point, but not under duress. Naively, the CFA offered to sponsor a radio broadcast, where they could freely testify about their politics. That plan went awry, however, when at least one of the witnesses told Philip Dunne that all of them either were now, or had recently been, communists. Worse, John Howard Lawson, the most ideologically rigid of the Hollywood Stalinists, in his testimony took an angry and patronizing tone in his exchanges with committee chairman J. Parnell Thomas, which cost the nineteen considerable sympathy, even among the liberal press.

It may have been very early in the Cold War, but public opinion was rapidly shifting from the live-and-let-live politics of the wartime popular front. The Soviet Union appeared to many to be hostile and threatening, and these feelings were fanned by the right-wing press of the day. There was almost no patience available to the communists. Their insistence on their absolute right to secrecy (which when tested in the courts was always struck down) quite quickly doomed their ability to work in the movies and began the shameful blacklist era.

More to our point, they almost doomed Humphrey Bogart's career. Very simply, he was the

Bacall and Bogart lead the Committee for the First Amendment in October 1947. Behind them are June Havoc and Danny Kaye.

"We weren't defending Communism (which in any case had not been outlawed), we were defending something else."

Lauren Bacall, *By Myself And Then Some*

most famous name the CFA recruited, and thus the perceived leader of their cause. He was also famously a "tough guy," unlike Kaye or Kelly. If he could be made to bend by the right it would be a tremendous victory for them. Moreover, he was vulnerable. *Dark Passage* had opened well in the early fall, but as the political drama in Washington played out, receipts dropped. And the expensive *Treasure* was due in the theaters in early 1948. Worse, he was in the midst of trying to set up an independent production company with Mark Hellinger and David O. Selznick and his political stance threatened that deal. But still, it was Jack Warner whose frenzy to get Bogart to recant was the most intense. This he refused to do—until, eventually, he did. At a between-trains press conference in Chicago on December 3, just days after the studios had issued their famous "Waldorf Statement" promising not to hire any unrepentant communists. "I went to Washington because I thought fellow Americans were deprived of their Constitutional Rights, and for that reason alone," Bogart said in a prepared statement. "That the trip was ill advised and foolish I am very ready to admit." He added that he "had no use for Communism nor for anyone who serves their philosophy." Bacall, when asked, concurred with everything he said. The press reveled in Bogart's behavior. Sperber and Lax quote one columnist writing: "All right, Humphrey. You can get up off your knees." They liked seeing famous movie stars, who had undertaken the political instruction of ordinary Americans, visibly groveling. For Bogart, that was pretty much it, though the following spring a piece under his by-line in *Modern Screen*, entitled "I'm No Communist," superfluously rehearsed his apology one last time.

Except, according to some of his friends, that was not quite the end of story. Richard Brooks went so far as to tell Sperber and Lax that thereafter he "was never the same again." Others, like Edward G. Robinson, felt sorry for a man obliged to live beneath the largely fictional façade of the character with which he had become identified. Bacall simply said "he never felt good about having made that statement."

Just how profoundly his failure of nerve affected Bogart is impossible to say. It certainly could, and should, be argued that the Hollywood communists had, by their tactics, sold out their liberal supporters, that he (and the rest of the CFA) had indeed been used by them, and that it was the better part of wisdom to renounce them once their strategy became clear. But that takes us into the realm of sophisticated political analysis that is beyond most show people. Bogart could only see that in a very public way he had not lived up to his image, that he had betrayed old-fashioned understanding that, in a free country, a man of principles could stand on them and court no more than controversy, certainly not calumny. For once, we might say, he had palpable reason to justify the air of rue he had for so long carried.

Still, life went on. By the spring he was at work again for Huston on a script largely written by Brooks, an adaptation of a Maxwell Anderson play called *Key Largo*, which in the end retained little more than the play's title. In it Bogart plays a man who has known better days, now seeking respite from the world (and the exactions of a liberal conscience) by making a

Time Out
A pause during shooting *The Big Sleep* with Bacall on her dressing-room step, Bogart lighting her cigarette.

visit to an isolated hotel in the Florida keys. His mission is to bring consolation to the widow (Lauren Bacall) and father (Lionel Barrymore) of his wartime friend, who was killed beside him in the Italian campaign. He feels he has done his bit in the fight against fascism during the war and is uninterested in taking arms against the breed in its native form, as personified by Edward G. Robinson, playing a particularly brutal mobster who, with his entourage, is in residence in the hotel. Bogart's fall here is less a social one than it is a descent from that special state of grace that moral rigor in the face of vulgar materialism is supposed to impart. Still, as *Casablanca* had led everyone to believe he always would, he eventually mobilizes himself and rids this little world of its oppressors just as he had previously helped rid the larger one of its dictators. It is not a bad movie, though there is a certain pomp in its writing, a certain mechanism in its structure. It is, though, better than Bogart's other films of the late forties, many of which were produced by his own company, Santana Productions. Pioneering independent production, most of them looked backward to the dying genres of the thirties and forties rather than forward to something new and different. It was not until 1950, with the release of *In a Lonely Place*, that Bogart offered something truly remarkable.

His portrayal of Dixon Steele, a screenwriter suspected of murder because everyone believes a man subject to his sudden fire storms of temper is surely capable of murder, represents an astonishing extension of his essential screen character into new and dangerous territory. Andrew Solt's screenplay, with its unique understanding of the hack Hollywood writer's temperament and his milieu, is brilliant, and Nicholas Ray's very claustrophobic direction—the film mostly takes place in a dark garden apartment complex—serves the script intelligently, flavorsomely, avoiding the mannered (and near-hysterical) fashion he sometimes embraced. But even though Dix Steele is a quintessential Ray figure, an outsider, a failure, and mentally disturbed, what gives the film its powerful authenticity is the fact that this character inhabits the world that Bogart himself knew intimately—the Los Angeles world of quiet bars and restaurants, lacking chic, where second-tier writers, small-time agents, minor character actors, foregather to exchange gossip and injustices and get soberly drunk.

Dix himself is not unlike Bogart. His WASPish name implies the possibility of a solid background, as do his manners, dress, and literate speech. To have ended up as a screenwriter is not what he expected, any more than Bogart imagined ending up as a screen actor. Moreover, Steele is now declassed in his profession as well. We understand that in the fairly recent past he was employed adapting serious fiction—or what Hollywood took to be serious fiction—to the screen and that he had been well regarded for his skills. When we meet him, however, he is not employed on much of anything—something to do with his personality. But in the opening sequence his faithful, long-suffering agent tracks him down in a bar, bearing a weighty tome, a trashy bestseller. He can get Steele the job adapting it if the writer can read the book overnight and the next day give his slant on the project to the producer. Grimly he agrees, then discovers the hatcheck girl in the restaurant has read the thing and is

Thinking Man
Bogart as troubled screenwriter Dixon Steele in Nicholas Ray's then underrated drama *In a Lonely Place* (1950).

agreeable to returning home with him to synopsize the plot verbally. She does, proves flirtatious, and is sent homeward by the writer in a cab. The next day we learn that she was murdered and that the police suspect Steele, largely because of his reputation for sudden and violent rages. A neighbor, Laurel Gray (very well played by Gloria Grahame, who was at the time married to Ray), provides Steele with an alibi, though it is not airtight, and the possibility that he might actually have been the killer lingers with both the police and the audience (apparently in one draft of the screenplay he was, in fact, the murderer). As the film traces the course of the love affair that develops between Dix and Laurel, she provides him with an emotional stability that permits him to work well on his new assignment—despite his troubles, he gets the adaptation job—but the growing jealousy with which he regards her and the rages that seem to come out of nowhere, triggered by the most trivial of incidents, destroy her love for him and enhance our suspicions of him right up to the bitterly ironic end, when another man confesses the murder, but Dix loses Laurel.

The plot is artfully braided, but it is the atmosphere in which it proceeds, and the psychological portrait of its central figure, that make the picture so haunting. The apartment house where Dix and Laurel live is perfect, one of those low, vaguely Spanish affairs, built around a courtyard, slightly shabby but still respectable, where, to this day, people on the way up and people on the way down in the movies find themselves. And Dix's digs are equally well realized. This is a true writer's lair—dark, clean, but carelessly strewn with the detritus a preoccupied man spreads in his wake. His favorite bar, the supporting players in his life, his social life with and without Laurel, are done with equally restrained intelligence—no sordidness, but never a note of false glamour to amuse the fans either.

It's a tough-minded movie, especially in the characterization of Steele. One type the movies never get right—the writer (for that matter, any creative person)—and another type they never touch—the angry man with no seeming motive for his anger—are efficiently struck off in the single figure of Dixon Steele. In an obituary column about Bogart, the drama critic John McClain, a drinking buddy, wrote: "He would much rather have made a modest living as a writer, where he could have aired his frustrations in print. He was a guy that didn't open up much, but the people he always sought out were writers ... they were the people for whom he had the most affection. In a funny way he was almost one of them."

Surely he was here. *In extremis*, it is probably fair to call Dix Steele a paranoid schizophrenic and therefore akin to Fred C. Dobbs. But this is that form of mental distress presented as we more often encounter it in life, possessing a man of breeding, education, intelligence. It is the glory of this script that it never introduces psychological testimony—no flashback-to-trauma to explain Steele's behavior. It is the glory of Bogart's performance that he never comments on that behavior. As far as he's concerned he's completely normal, which is why he's so completely chilling in the part. This was rare at a time when Hollywood had discovered mental illness as a topic and performers of every type were desperately seeking to

Practical Man
Bogart won his only Oscar for his portrayal of Charlie
Allnut in John Huston's huge hit *The African Queen* (1951).

enlist our sympathies in psychological tragedy. The picture trusts the audience to catch its understated drift and Bogart's performance, summarizing all the solitaries he played in the past, drains that figure of all romance.

In a sense Bogart completed his life's work here. In the six active years left to him he added nothing essential to his screen character. Still, there were yet some good things for him to do, most notably the film that remains, next to *Casablanca*, his most widely beloved work, *The African Queen*. It is, of course, a "fighting romance" (to borrow the old-fashioned Hollywood phrase) and the casting of Katharine Hepburn, spunky and full of her sweet arrogance as always, opposite Bogart, typically withdrawn and calculating, would have been inspired in any case. But his Charlie Allnut was a very able variation on his Fred C. Dobbs. They were at heart similar figures, drifters on civilization's farthest fringes. But Charlie's suspiciousness is well founded; a rational man confronting Hepburn's plans for escape from known perils by embracing the unknown ones of a river voyage aboard the eponymous rust bucket, he is entitled to his skepticism. Today, the thing seems too cute by half, but at the time it seemed funny and oddly touching under Huston's direction, and by now Bogart's service to Hollywood was lengthy enough to assure him of the 1952 Academy Award. If he had been better, perhaps, in other pictures, this one was big and splashy and readily adorable and thus, by Hollywood standards, a suitable occasion to celebrate not just a performance but his life's achievements.

Immediately after that there was *Deadline – U.S.A.*, Richard Brooks's newspaper yarn in which—again a gentleman in raffish waters—Bogart plays the editor of a newspaper the heirs to which wish to sell it to a chain, silencing its independent crusading voice. In the course of the picture he demonstrates his ability to speak many languages: That of a tough professional in a tough craft; that of the trusted servitor of the *grande dame* whose husband founded the sheet (she is played by Ethel Barrymore, and their scenes demonstrate Bogart's good breeding as well as any he ever had); that of a conventional hero standing up to mob threats; that of a lover whose duties keep diverting him from romantic obligations.

On the whole, his next—and last—picture with Huston, *Beat the Devil*, is for sophisticated tastes more entertaining than *The African Queen*, though Bogart's role is straighter, more reactive—the still center of some truly divine lunacy. In terms of his overall career it is interesting largely because it is the last time he plays a gentleman fallen from social grace. Indeed, his Billy Dannreuther, trim in blazers and ascots, might well be Rick Blaine a decade later. An American expatriate, he has, until recently, lived well on the proceeds of various mysterious schemes—a great villa he once owned near Ravello, Italy (where the picture was shot), is shown; a grand car that was once his is displayed in the course of the story. Now, alas, down on his luck, he is reduced to helping an ill-assorted crowd of swindlers, led by Robert Morley (in a gorgeous display of pomp and menace), obtain mining concessions in "British East." He and his crowd have at least cornered the market in comically stated paranoia, and it is Bogart who here represents the reality principle, not only to them but also

Last Orders
Bogart in the final film he made with John Huston, here directing him, the whimsical spoof *Beat the Devil* (1953).

to an Englishwoman (Jennifer Jones, in a blond wig and in the performance of her life), whose dottiness takes the form of compulsive lying and excessive romanticism. The picture apparently started out to be a straight melodrama, in the international intrigue genre; but it was entirely too routine in that form for Huston's taste, and Truman Capote was brought in to rewrite it with him. The result was a great shaggy dog story, deliriously, but with marvelously straight face, sending up the conventions of the glamour-thriller. And a field day for a cast happily parodying themselves—except for Bogart, whose company produced the picture. He didn't particularly enjoy the joke or the cult that formed around the picture, and he especially did not enjoy its commercial fate; it was a box-office disaster.

But if *Beat the Devil* was too special in its appeal for mass-market success, Bogart was still on a good roll, exemplified by *The Caine Mutiny*. With its worrying over the question of duty in a democracy, it was a middlebrow movie *par excellence*, but Bogart was excellent as the paranoiac Captain Queeg—Fred C. Dobbs and Dix Steele crammed into a professional naval officer's uniform. Looking at it now, one also sees a prefiguration of Richard Nixon, with his tense rigidity masked by false good cheer in the film's early passages, the descent into lunacy as the pressures of command begin to reach his quaking soul in its later ones. In any event, Bogart's witness-stand breakdown is as good a scene as he ever played, and since he is playing (as the saying goes) a gentleman by act of Congress, and since the highly dubious moral of the Herman Wouk novel under adaptation is that gentlemanly dutifulness is the backbone of the Republic, it perhaps suited his mood—the country's mood at the time—admirably.

A few months later Bogart appeared in Billy Wilder's *Sabrina*, this time, for the first time, playing a gentleman who is not the least bit declassed. As the responsible eldest son of a great family, a dour man in a black suit and a homburg, he soberly permits his raffish father and his playboy younger brother all the fun while he attends their vast holdings. He does, in the course of the film, permit himself to be declassed emotionally. For in trying to extricate his brother from an affair with their chauffeur's daughter (Audrey Hepburn) Bogart's character falls in love with her, and he extracts good humor from his belated efforts to loosen up and lighten up. In this picture one imagines him imagining all those stage juveniles of his Broadway past— sobered up by thirty years of life, but given a chance to rediscover something of their lost youths. Some people thought he was a little old to be romancing Hepburn, but she was, in fact, only five years younger than Bacall and that had worked out all right, hadn't it?

The pictures he made thereafter are, I think, best left in something like near-silence. He was the mouthpiece of Joseph Mankiewicz's incorrigible gliberalism in *The Barefoot Contessa*, a literate (and, of course, gentlemanly) film director commenting sardonically on the bad values of the business and of its allies in the international set; an escaped convict in a misbegotten comedy, *My Three Angels*, an overwrought gangster leading his mob into improbable refuge in a middle-class family's home (a reversion to his least successful type) in *The Desperate Hours*; a downed flier disguising himself as a priest to escape a Chinese

Bogart's Prefiguration of Nixon
His portrayal of Captain Queeg, paranoid master of USS *Caine*, suggests a kinship with the scandalous Watergate president.

warlord in *The Left Hand of God*; an out-of-work sportswriter—again a man of obvious breeding and better than his surroundings, of course—drawn into a scheme to promote an inept prizefighter to championship status in *The Harder They Fall*. All of these efforts, in accordance with the witless spirit of the American 1950s, imposed "thoughtful" themes on melodramatic and generic stories for the sober consideration of the middlebrow audience. They provided him with lecture topics, but they lacked the livewire energy of Hollywood moviemaking when it was young and full of careless rapture. In this period he was saying, with considerable justification, "I'm a professional. I've done pretty well, don't you think? I've survived in a pretty rough business." According to Alistair Cooke he never spoke of art, which would have seemed pretentious, even grandiloquent to him, only of craft.

On the night he won his Oscar for *The African Queen* his wife could not help reflecting that "Bogie had everything now—a happy marriage, a son, another child on the way, an ocean racing yawl, success, and the peak of recognition in his work." Some wondered, why in the light of that accomplishment, he kept doing at least one film per year. But he still believed that the more one did of it, the better the chances for a lucky accident to occur. Moreover, it provided a distraction from the brooding that idleness entailed. Finally, he became, in these years, mildly obsessed with providing a legacy for his young wife and their children.

He developed what seems a telling habit during this period. Annually, on Christmas Eve, he would invite some friends over for a bibulous screening of *A Star Is Born*, which, according to reliable witnesses, usually ended with Bogart dissolved in sentimental tears. One has to think that in contemplating the sad fate of Norman Maine, the movie star who succumbs to alcoholism and suicide in that film, Bogart may have been contemplating his own good fortune in narrowly escaping a similarly miserable end. For certainly there were parallels in their stories that went far beyond their addiction to booze: The air they projected of being finer than their surroundings, their contempt for Hollywood manners and morals, their redemptive love for a young woman star in whose discovery they participated. Given the self-contempt that continually shadowed him, he might well have ended up a Hollywood footnote of the order of the fictional Maine, someone who feels entirely unworthy of the unearned increments of fame and fortune that are mysteriously granted a lucky few, so perhaps he was sobbing with relief at the fate he had avoided, this reserved and uncommunicative man, now at last gratefully enjoying the perquisites of success and celebrity, but not flaunting them.

He had become, via an unlikely and circuitous route, what birth and breeding had intended him all along to be and what circumstances, as he thought, had denied him: He was, at last, a perfect gentleman—prosperous and well-regarded in his profession, blessed by a happy family, warmed by the high regard of friends, able to pursue his interests in chess and sailing and the perusal of good books well away from the madding, growing crowd of celebrity worshipers. It is the bitterest of ironies that he did not live to enjoy the fullness of his years in hard-earned peacefulness. But the luck that had come to him so late in life ran out early

Previous Pages **Uneasy Teaming**
Bogart cared little for his *Sabrina* co-star Audrey Hepburn, even less for William Holden, nor was he wild about director Billy Wilder.

At the Helm
Bogart loved sailing, and was never happier than when steering his yacht *Santana* on Pacific waters.

in his life, with the onslaught of cancer (of the esophagus, which so often takes people who combine alcohol and tobacco in prodigious amounts). Yet it might be argued that nothing so became him in life as his manner of leaving it. Never once in the long months that he fought his illness did he hint that it was more than a temporary thing. He kept insisting, indeed, that all he needed to effect a recovery was the return of enough strength so that he could resume work. Though scarcely able to eat, he was stoic and gallant in a quiet way that has been remembered and admired as exemplary by everyone who witnessed his last year. Both John Huston and Alistair Cooke have, in fact, drawn unforgettable portraits of him in that time. It became the habit of his friends to drop in casually for brief visits at the end of the day. Bogart would be shaved and dressed in gray flannels and a red smoking jacket in his upstairs bedroom, then placed in a wheelchair and transferred to a dumbwaiter, which carried him to the first floor. Then he would be transferred to another wheelchair and taken to his den, where, drink in hand and a cigarette glowing, he would await his callers, each of whom would stay for a half hour or so. He continued to relish the industry gossip they brought to him. Around eight, after they had all left, he would be returned to his room by the same painful route he had left it. As Huston put it when he eulogized him, "No one who sat in his presence during those final weeks will ever forget. It was a unique display of sheer animal courage. After the first visit—the visit was spent getting over the initial shock—one quickened to the grandeur of it, expanded and felt strangely elated, proud to be there ... the friend of such a brave man...."

It was, of course, acting. The show of courage always is. But it was acting of the special kind on which his fame had rested and his legend would continue to rest. He was dying as a gentleman must. Without complaint. With dignity. With his emotions under control and with thoughts spared for the feelings of friends and loved ones. At the end he was perhaps more in touch with his essence, clinging to it, believing in it, than he had ever been. He would let no one down—least of all himself. He died in his sleep on January 14, 1957.

"The whole world is three drinks behind. If everybody in the world would take three drinks, we would have no trouble. Of course, it should be handled in moderation. You should be able to handle it. I don't think it should handle you. But that's what the world needs, three more drinks."

Humphrey Bogart

Home Sweet Home
The picture is absurd and intended to be, a parody of the worst "stars-at-home" images suggesting a healthy outdoor life.

The Movies

George Perry

Two mischievous jokes of fate informed the birth of Humphrey DeForest Bogart. The first was the day itself, Christmas Day 1899, which would deny him the innocent childhood joy of having his birthday to himself. Sadly, Christmas children become all too aware that the adult mentality cannot comprehend a necessity to dispense a double order of presents to those so unfortunately blighted. In some reference books, and even official Warner Bros. biographies, is the indication that he was actually born on January 23, 1899. There is enough documentary evidence, including two census returns and his school records, to show this to be wrong and to confirm December 25 as the true date.

His second unfortunate accident of birth is that although the persona that he would project so successfully seemed to suggest that he was someone who had hauled himself by the bootstraps out of a deprived urban slum in the conventional rags-to-riches fulfillment of the American dream, in truth his parents were monied, privileged and individually successful, and so he never had the need to struggle financially. The childhood home was an elegant brownstone at 245 West 103rd Street, off West End Avenue and a block from Riverside Drive, which then, before the development of Park Avenue, was as chic an address as any to be found in New York. There was also a 55-acre family property at Seneca Point on Lake Canandaigua near Rochester in the upper part of the state.

His father, Belmont DeForest Bogart, his lineage going back to the Dutch burghers of New Amsterdam, was a surgeon, a heart and lung specialist with many wealthy patients. When an intern, soon after graduating from medical school at Columbia, a horse-drawn ambulance toppled on him, and his broken leg was badly set, giving him pain for the rest of his life. His approach to life was much more passive than that of the woman he married in 1898, the formidable Maud Humphrey, who had studied art in Paris alongside James McNeill Whistler, and had become the highest-paid woman illustrator and painter in America. In the 1890s she was earning an astonishing $50,000 a year, which in modern terms would be well over a million dollars. She was the dominant force in the family, a woman not given to undue sentimentality. Her son would call her "Maud," but would address her husband as "Father." While leaving little Humphrey to be raised by nursemaids she nevertheless put his cherubic infant image to use, allowing her drawing of him to be applied to the advertising and products of Mellin's Baby Foods. In later life he said: "There was a period in American history when you couldn't pick up a goddamed magazine without seeing my kisser in it."

Two sisters were born after Humphrey. Frances, generally known as Pat, came in 1901 and Katherine, or Kay, in 1903. Both were to have unhappy destinies. Pat became insane and Kay an alcoholic who died at only thirty-four. Maud, who would also later have moments of mental instability, tended to tog out her son in affected Fauntleroy outfits with frilly shirts and velvet breeches, which combined with the effete-sounding name "Humphrey" set him apart from more robustly attired boys of his own age. In spite of its wealth and status his family was not a model of stability. In a household not given to excesses of emotion his affections were mainly directed toward his much more easygoing father, who was developing into a morphine addict on account of his injury. He at least taught his son to sail on Lake Canandaigua, giving him a taste for the water that never left him. Sadly, his childhood was conditioned by memories of huddling under blankets with his sisters in the upstairs nursery in a vain attempt to shut out the sounds of their parents' quarreling.

He was initially sent to a private Upper West Side school, De Lancey, and moved after fourth grade to Trinity School, founded in 1709 and the oldest private establishment in New York. Although favored by the rich, it was an austere place, modeled on English public schools and dedicated, as was demonstrated by its motto *Fides Labore et Virtute* ("Faith through work and virtue"), into preparing its students for eventual admission to the Ivy League colleges. Among its famous alumni after Bogart was Truman Capote. Young Humphrey spent eight years there, excelling in neither studies nor sports, and was absent without authorization many times. Even school dramatics were of no interest to him. His mother, however hopeless the idea, cherished the ambition that he would somehow find himself, and make it to Yale. With that prospect in mind he was moved on to his father's alma mater, the prestigious prep school Phillips Academy in Andover, Massachusetts, an academic powerhouse.

By that time the family fortunes had waned considerably as a consequence of his father's bad investments, and the Seneca Point house had gone, a rented summer cottage on Fire Island its replacement, but it was the connections, and not his academic grades, that secured his place. It was impossible, however, for his continued indifference to the scholastic regime to be ignored and before the academic year was up he was asked to leave, to the bitter disappointment of his parents. His mother made it clear that he was on his own from then on, and he would have to find a job. As World War I was in progress he enlisted in the Navy, reporting for duty on July 2, 1918 at the Naval Reserve station at Pelham Park in the Bronx. After many weeks of training he was assigned to a ship, the U.S.S. *Leviathan*, which had formerly been a German troopship, the *Vaterland*. Seaman Bogart was to see no action. Two days later the Armistice signaled the end of the conflict, and for the next eight months he was in the crew on about a dozen transatlantic trips ferrying tired doughboys back from the battlefields.

Even serving in the armed forces had not altered his attitude toward authority, and his service record was far from spotless. His shore leaves were often curtailed, and he found himself in the brig for arguing with an officer. During his Navy days he also sustained the injury to his upper lip that left a permanent scar and partial paralysis, and gave him the characteristic lisp that added interest to his performances. How it came about has never been satisfactorily explained. One version has it that it was caused by splinters from an exploding shell, which seems unlikely as he never put to sea until well after hostilities had ended. Another claims that he was escorting a manacled defaulter at Boston South Station en route for Portsmouth Naval Prison. The prisoner had escaped by smashing the chain into his face. Bogart, in spite of the blood, was still able to down him in flight with a well-placed gunshot. That too, seems too highly colored to be credible. In any case, an injury incurred on active duty would have led to compensation and even a small pension. The medical officer responsible for stitching him did not do a very good job, and the work had to be rectified years later by his father just as he was about to make his first film.

Seaman Second Class Bogart was honorably discharged on June 18, 1919. His father's practice had by now dwindled, in part due to his increasing morphine dependence. For a short time his son worked as a runner for Strauss and Co., his family's investment brokers, and then, with his naval experience an advantage, for the Pennsylvania Tug and Lighterage Company as an inspector tracing lost shipments. A story has it that his boss told him to work hard and he could become president, but when he discovered that there were some fifty thousand other employees between him and that exalted position he quit.

It was then that he entered the theater business. A neighbor on nearby Riverside Drive was a colorful Broadway producer and early filmmaker, William A. Brady. His daughter Alice, born in 1892, had become an established star of the silent screen. His son Bill Brady Jr. was Humphrey's age, and his boyhood best friend. It was a connection that undoubtedly led to his employment as Brady Sr.'s office boy and general assistant, and the beginning of his professional career.

He was now twenty. In spite of a privileged background his young life had been singularly undistinguished. He had failed to shine in sports as well as his studies and had been thrown out of one of America's best schools for not working. He had not been to university. His spell in the Navy had been lackluster. He seemed to have no ambition or a clear sense of direction.

Yet he was to become one of the greatest of all Hollywood actors, his iconic image persisting long after his death and the fading from memory of his even more celebrated contemporaries. Moreover, his reputation never depended on his looks, but on the force of his exceptional talent, the intelligence, subtlety and depth he brought to his performances. He was a slow starter. By the time he attained his stardom he was in his forties, had been working in films for over a decade, and had been acting for twenty years. Across twenty-five years he made nearly eighty films, some of which (*The Maltese Falcon*, *Casablanca*, *The Big Sleep*, *The Treasure of the Sierra Madre*, *The African Queen*) are unassailable classics, together with several others that are memorable and important, among them *High Sierra*, *To Have and Have Not*, *Key Largo*, *In a Lonely Place* and *The Caine Mutiny*. Even so, the majority of his output, especially in his pre-stardom days, is dismal routine stuff, in which he is either so relegated in billing position as to be almost inconspicuous, or so scandalously misused by script, casting, and direction that his presence is embarrassingly inappropriate. It was of course the fate of the contract player to do as he or she was bidden, and the system was ruthless in eliminating or bypassing those who objected. Bogart was also driven by the notion that it was better to keep busy than not. William Brady's wife, the actress Grace George, had said to him: "Always keep working. Never be available. By constant working you learn the business." He followed that precept. He was no overnight sensation, his ascendancy took time and patience, and when it was achieved he remained at the top until he died.

His first experience of the movie world occurred in 1920 when he was working for Brady as production manager at the Peerless Studios across the Hudson River at Fort Lee, New Jersey, at the considerable salary for a twenty-year-old of $50 a week. For some reason the director of a film called *Life*, starring Rod La Roque and Arlene Pretty, was fired, and Brady asked Bogart to add to his duties of renting the props and furnishings, and paying the actors, by finishing the film himself. The results were so inept that Brady himself had to take over. Yet although directing clearly was not Bogart's forte, he was attracted to the movies, a passion that went back a long time. With Brady's son he had spent many a school afternoon playing truant to watch films in the neighborhood movie theater, and was now delighted at an opportunity to be involved in their gestation, even if the technicalities were beyond his competence. He next tried his hand at writing, and fashioned a lurid screenplay "full of blood and death," which Brady thought interesting enough to pass on to Jesse L. Lasky, a prominent producer and partner of Cecil B. DeMille. Lasky gave it to Walter Wanger, an assistant, to read, and he ditched it in disgust. Years later, having become a Hollywood producer, he would boast that Bogart had once written for him.

Brady's wife, Grace George, then invited him to go on the road with her as stage manager for a play called *A Ruined Lady*, a six-month tour that would introduce him to the joys of theatrical boarding and wrestling with stages in unfamiliar towns. His duties not only included making sure that the production was in order, but also in an emergency being ready to go on himself to

Hollywood Greenhorn
Humphrey Bogart in 1930, the year he made his tentative, lackluster Hollywood debut.

play a role. Such an occasion arose. The juvenile lead fell ill and Bogart had to fill his shoes at short notice. Having previously derided the actor for having an easy job against his own, that of merely having to mouth words that had already been written, he found the experience of being in front of an audience terrifying. Perhaps it was for the best that his debut occurred on the last night of the tour.

In May 1921 he was given another chance, appearing in an Alice Brady play at Fulton Theater in Brooklyn, as a Japanese houseboy delivering one line while holding a drinks tray. His father saw him and exclaimed: "The boy's good, isn't he?" Nobody had the heart to tell him the contrary. The Bradys persisted, undeterred. On January 2, 1922 Humphrey Bogart made his first appearance on Broadway in *Drifting*, a play directed by John Cromwell, again starring Alice Brady. The part was so minor that it was not mentioned in any of the reviews, but the play was dismissed as a "flashy melodrama." In June he took over a part in *Up the Ladder*, another Brady production, and by October he had blossomed into second lead in *Swifty*, starring Frances Howard and Neil Hamilton, with Cromwell directing, playing "a young sprig of the aristocracy." He was still not well received, although Cromwell patiently coped with his acting inexperience, but the play lasted a mere three weeks.

Bogart gave acting a rest after that and concentrated on other duties for Brady. As a young man with a good salary and a taste for the socializing that seemed to electrify New York in the Prohibition era, he also went out with actresses, drank with sports writers, hung out in numerous clubs and speakeasies, sailed on Long Island Sound, danced until dawn, and sharpened his skills at chess, a cerebral game which he infinitely preferred to playing golf.

In November 1923 he was back on Broadway, playing a reporter in *Meet the Wife* starring Mary Boland, a prominent stage diva, and the urbane Clifton Webb, who was to become a good friend. Bogart was now earning $150 a week in a play that would run for 232 performances, and the critics, while acclaiming the leads, also noted the refreshing charm he brought to his lesser role. Even Alexander Woolcott, who had previously derided him as "inadequate," admitted that he had misjudged him earlier. Unfortunately, he slightly tarnished his name near the end of the run by blowing his lines as a consequence of having caroused too heavily the night before, and after the curtain had fallen he was bawled out in front of the cast by a furious Boland, who vowed never to work with him again, although she later relented.

He clearly had a quality that appealed to audiences. His stage persona was smooth, clean-cut and fresh-faced. His voice was strong and distinctive, the rasp and slight lisp already becoming a recognizable trademark. Slight-of-build but muscular, he had sleek, dark hair, a firm jawline and pleasant, open features, only slightly marred by his lip scar. His bearing and manners were those of a well-raised, young man-about-town, the sort of character in the drawing-room comedies of the day who would breeze on to the stage in a blazer and whites, with a racket under his arm, and say "Tennis, anyone?" Bogart claimed to be the originator of this theatrical cliché, supposedly invented by playwrights as a device to clear the set of unnecessary cast members so that the leads could get on with their love scene.

During a tour of *Drifting* Alice Brady, who was pregnant, suddenly had to withdraw when she went into premature labor, and all through a hectic weekend another actress in the cast, Helen Menken, rehearsed the part from scratch, ready to appear on Monday. She had been acting since childhood and was much more experienced than Bogart, but they had become such good friends that he had taken out a marriage licence. It was not actually used for a considerable time, but after more plays, his acceptance and recognition by audiences and critics, and her success in *Seventh Heaven*, he found that the arguments for marrying her were becoming pressing. She had a glittering career, fabulous contacts and was very anxious to become his wife. What clinched it was that his friend Bill Brady, by now married to a young actress, told him: "If you don't marry that girl you'll never get another part on Broadway."

On May 20, 1926 a strange ceremony took place at the Gramercy Park Hotel, attended by the elite of the theater world. The bride's parents were both deaf, as was the officiating Episcopalian cleric, and the event was conducted in sign language. For the benefit of those with normal hearing the minister also spoke the service in the muffled, shrieking diction of someone who could not hear himself, bringing a note of bizarre horror to what should have been a joyous occasion. When it was concluded, the bride, on the verge of hysteria, declined to speak to the press.

It was a brief union, as though foredoomed. Their careers in different plays continued, and on the domestic front there was much quarreling. The breaking point came when Bogart was offered a part in the Chicago production of the Maxwell Anderson play *Saturday's Children*, which he had already performed in New York. Menken absolutely refused to leave New York, and they separated, at first tentatively. Eventually she sought a divorce and went to London to play *Seventh Heaven* there. In later life both blamed themselves for the marital breakdown, and it was a case on both sides of putting career first.

In actual fact he did not remain unmarried for long. He had become attracted to another actress, Mary Philips, who was then twenty-five, having met her during the run of *Meet the Wife*. They were married on April 3, 1928 in Hartford, Connecticut at her mother's house. In another part of the state, at Fairfield, they rented a country home, close to Stuart Rose, who had been his long-term friend as well as brother-in-law, as he had married Pat, Bogart's sister. He had also been best man at his marriage to Helen Menken. The following winter Bogart and his second wife were teamed together in a play called *Skyrocket*, about a young married couple who acquire a fortune and become miserable, then lose it and become happy again.

The tone seemed to prefigure the Wall Street Crash which occurred at the end of October, 1929. Bogart was at that time appearing in a comedy produced by David Belasco, *It's a Wise Child*, which turned out to be his biggest stage hit, lasting for 378 performances. The stock-market collapse had severely affected his father, whose fortunes had been in a slow decline as

his son's had risen. As his medical practice had waned and his incapacity increased Dr. Bogart had been living off his wife's income, although they now lived at separate addresses. Yet Maud paid for his nurses, cooked his breakfast, sat with him for hours, then went home to her own apartment. There was no thought of divorce in such an unusual marriage, which was remarkable for the extraordinary resilience and toughness of Mrs. Bogart.

The new economic conditions also had a serious effect on movies. The brothers Warner, bucking the notion that there was no future in talkies, had effectively launched *The Jazz Singer*, which contrary to popular belief, was a largely silent film, with a few songs performed in lip sync by Al Jolson, but without dialogue apart from some ad-libbed remarks uttered while he was strumming the piano keys. The crowds besieged the Warners' Theater on Broadway and 51st, and the film had a catastrophic impact on silent movies. During 1928 they were rendered obsolescent as studios hastily wired up for recording, and grafted sound sequences on to silent films awaiting release. By 1929 the silent picture was completely superseded, submerged by a floodtide of indifferent, statically photographed, talking dramas and indifferently staged musicals so lacking in cinematic imagination they might as well have been shot from a theater auditorium. The cost of installing sound equipment had driven theater owners as well as Hollywood producers to the edge of bankruptcy, and the stock-market crash made conditions much worse all round.

In Hollywood the studios also made the horrifying discovery that many of the most prominent stars of the silent screen had never learned vocal projection, or were blighted by thick regional accents and flat, nasal delivery far beyond the healing capability of any voice coach. Some were able to make the transition and adapted to the new medium, but many found their careers had run into a brick wall and oblivion. Consequently New York theaters were haunted by desperate talent scouts dispatched from California to look out for suitably photogenic candidates who knew how to speak their lines clearly and acceptably. The biggest lure was money, which was paid out at a rate almost unheard of in the theater. Less appealing to stage actors were the working conditions. Playing to a camera was very different from a live performance before an organic, responding audience, and acting technique was of another order. What may have seemed effective within a proscenium arch became over-blown and unnatural on screen, and performances had to be toned down by several notches to become acceptable. An actor used to weeks of rehearsal to develop a role found that a scene would be shot after only two or three run-throughs, often completely out of sequence with the plot. A stage actor could control, hone and develop a performance. The screen actor was at the mercy of the director, cinematographer and above all, the editor, who could destroy best efforts in the cutting-room. So the traffic was not one-way. Many hopefuls found the movie business, in spite of financial inducements, too hard to master, and retreated back to New York.

Bogart was among those young actors who were spotted and considered. He even appeared in a New York two-reeler called *The Dancing Town*, which starred Helen Hayes. Unfortunately

Second Try
The young Bogart in *Nerves* with Paul Kelly and Mary Philips, from 1928 his second wife.

the film is lost, and little is known about it. Another, a one-reel film shot in Brooklyn for the Vitaphone *Varieties* series of program fillers, has fared slightly better. Appearing with him were Joan Blondell, Mary Philips and the quivering torch singer Ruth Etting who warbled "The Right Kind of Man" and "From the Bottom of My Heart." Characteristically, Bogart had a lady-killing role. The ten-minute film has been found, but is minus its soundtrack, although other Etting Vitaphone shorts of the period that have survived are feeble and unchallenging. Bogart was tested on more than one occasion for Hollywood, but he found that his rigid upper lip, with its curious polyp-like protrusion on the right side, which went unnoticed in live performance, turned out to be a distraction for the camera, with its ruthless propensity to examine faces in close-up. He asked his father to perform some corrective surgery, greatly improving his prospects. Stuart Rose, who was then working for Fox in their New York office as story editor, managed to get a test approved, and Bogart was put on contract for a handsome $750 a week, a huge improvement on his Broadway earnings. Mary, who was in a play on Broadway, refused to accompany him to Los Angeles, a career decision that he was in no position to fault given that he was behaving with equal ruthlessness where his marriage was concerned.

"Bogie was not great in these films – but then, the films weren't great either. In some he was good, in others lousy. He did, however, get good at dramatic death scenes because he had lots of practice. In these gangster films he was always getting knocked off at the end by Robinson or Cagney. He joked about how absurd it was that he, brought up in wealth and culture, was known to the public as a tough street guy. But he was not happy playing these parts. He really cared about acting, and he wanted to make something of himself as an actor."

Stephen Bogart, *Bogart: In Search of my Father*

1930 – 1939

Humphrey Bogart's first Hollywood foray did not go swimmingly. Expecting to play the lead in *The Man Who Came Back*, he was surprised to find two other actors also had that belief, but it was always going to be an established star, Charles Farrell, who would get it. Bogart was given the job of coaching him to say his lines properly. He was then put into two films shot back-to-back, as a wealthy young adventurer alongside Victor McLaglen in *A Devil with Women*, and as a convict in one of John Ford's worst films, *Up the River*, where for the only time he played in a film with Spencer Tracy, also making a debut. Bogart was then in a supporting role with Farrell starring in *Body and Soul*, and next loaned to Universal for *Bad Sister*, Bette Davis's first film. Both she and Bogart were told by Carl Laemmle Jr., who ran production for his father's studio, that they had no future in movies. After two more Fox flops Bogart scurried back to New York, chastened.

The Depression had hit Broadway badly and new productions were few. He was lucky to find a part in John Van Druten's *After All* with Helen Haye (not to be confused with Hayes), but left during the run, returning to Hollywood with a new contract at Columbia. It was another false dawn, but on loan to Warner he played a gangster for the first time in *Three on a Match*. Disappointed by low billing he again retreated to New York, but times were now so hard he was sometimes reduced to playing chess or bridge for money. His father's health and wealth were gone, one sister was an alcoholic, the other an acute manic depressive. His wife was also drinking too much, and neither of them slowed their intake with the repeal of the Volstead Act. He was in two or three short runs on Broadway, and played a gangster in *Midnight*, a Universal film made in New York.

A turning point came when he was cast to play Duke Mantee, the Dillinger-like escaped killer in *The Petrified Forest* on Broadway. His triumph was marred on a personal level when shortly after its opening his father died. A massive hit, the play closed prematurely because its star, the English actor Leslie Howard, wanted a vacation in Scotland. A film was in preparation and Howard expected Bogart to be in it. Warner, however, named Edward G. Robinson. Howard refused to appear without Bogart, so both repeated their Broadway roles.

On his third crack at Hollywood Bogart was now established, but not as a star. His position was that of dependable contract actor. While he could now join the elite group of Warner heavies: Robinson, Cagney, and Raft, he was of lesser status, and when not playing mobsters, convicts, and hatchet men, he had many unsuitable roles in hastily assembled pictures, a hoe-down musical for instance, and a couple of westerns, even a horror movie. The studio head, Jack Warner, kept up output relentlessly, and in the days of double bills a constant flow of

Headline Grabbing
Bogart in *Black Legion* (1937), a Warner social-conscience movie concerning xenophobic labor disputes.

lesser films was necessary. Not that Bogart accepted such dross without protest. He was among a select group, including Bette Davis, who fought bitterly against the enslaving aspects of the studio system, and endured several suspensions. Among his better films was *Dead End*, directed by William Wyler. Occasionally he was given a part on the other side of the law, perhaps as a crusading district attorney. In *Stand-In* he connived with his friend Leslie Howard to mock the film industry itself. Meanwhile, his marriage foundered. Mary Philips preferred New York, and embarked on an affair with the British actor Roland Young. The divorce occurred on June 21, 1938.

James Cagney had said that not many people liked Bogart and he knew it. Bogart was admired for integrity and concern for his craft, and his disdain for Hollywood hoop-la, but was never regarded as a social animal. He made a point of finishing work at six to go home. Gossip columnists who managed to catch up with him were often fed misinformation.

He had an old-fashioned propensity for marrying the women in whom he was interested. His romance with Mayo Methot erupted quickly. She had a small role in *Marked Woman*, in which Bogart played an attorney, with Bette Davis a "hostess." Mayo and Bogie married on August 20, 1938. He was her third husband, she was his third wife. He soon found that however sweet and adoring when sober, drunk she was a violent, jealous termagant, and the first woman who could out-drink him. Visitors to their house never quite knew what to expect, and their vicious, unashamed warring earned them the title "the battling Bogarts." He called her "Sluggy," applying the same name to the powerboat he bought so that they could float off to Catalina at weekends.

With *Racket Busters* he at last achieved top billing. He appeared with Cagney in *Angels With Dirty Faces* as a shady lawyer. Then he was in the sagebrush in *The Oklahoma Kid*, a western in which he and Cagney were badmen but Bogart was worse, and *The Roaring Twenties*, where he was the racketeer who successfully rode the Wall Street Crash, to die from Cagney's gunshots. In *Brother Orchid* he remained the hard man when Edward G. Robinson quit gangsterdom for a monastery, and in *They Drive by Night* he and George Raft were cast as Californian independent truckers, struggling to stay beyond the reach of the vehicle repossessor. Bogart lost an arm in a crash and faded from view, leaving Raft the rest of the plot involving the attempt by an infatuated Ida Lupino to incriminate him for the murder of her husband. The studio seemed unable to see that Bogart was in an entirely different league to the spiritless Raft, the most limited of the Warner tough guys. Without realizing it, Raft was about to make a number of career mistakes that propelled Bogart into full stardom.

Peaceful Moment
Domestic bliss seems delicately posed, as third wife Mayo Methot pours Bogart's morning tea.

Up the River (1930)

The film debut of both Humphrey Bogart and Spencer Tracy, and the only time these later close friends appeared in a film together, is inauspicious stuff for them both, in spite of John Ford's direction. Originally intended as a heavy prison drama, it was reworked as a comedy by Maurine Watkins, who was the originator of the much-adapted *Chicago*, and shot in a mere two weeks. Claire Luce, also making a debut, plays a prisoner in the women's wing, and Bogart is a mild-mannered parolee rescued from a crook threatening to expose him by Tracy and Warren Hymer who escape specially for that purpose, then return to help the prison baseball team achieve victory. Not exactly Ford's shining hour.

A Devil With Women (1930)

Victor McLaglen plays a rugged soldier of fortune in a Latin-American country hired to smoke out a notorious bandit leader, and Bogart is a brash, well-connected young turk who constantly irks him, especially where senoritas are concerned. They both nearly get shot by a firing squad, but McLaglen succeeds in getting his man, Bogart, the girl, and both men sink their differences. A modest film in most respects, it features Bogart in one of his debonair, upper-crust roles in which he was stereotyped on Broadway.

Mona Maris and Bogart in *A Devil With Women*.

Body and Soul (1931)

Charles Farrell was the star of this World War II action drama set in France. Both he and Bogart are among a group of American aviators attached to the Royal Air Force, but the latter's role is abruptly terminated when he is shot down and killed while attempting to destroy an enemy balloon. Although Bogart's screen time is limited, the role is pivotal to the plot, with Farrell spending much of the rest of the film unraveling the dead pilot's complicated love life.

"I spent a very unsuccessful year at Fox." Humphrey Bogart on his first six films

Donal Dillaway, Bogart, and Charles Farrell, *Body and Soul*.

Bad Sister (1931)

Another smooth role for Bogart, and a remake of a silent film. He plays a conman who comes to a small Midwest town and endeavors to secure backing for a non-existent factory. Sidney Fox, in her debut, plays a local siren who falls for his charm and elopes with him after forging her father's signature. Her wallflower sister (Bette Davis, also making her first film) marries the local doctor (Conrad Nagel) who was previously smitten by her glamorous sibling. It is an undistinguished work, but Bogart would work with both actresses again to much better effect. Both Davis and Bogart were told that they were lackluster performers and that there was no future for them at Universal.

Women of all Nations (1931)

Not much of a career advancement for Bogart in this postwar reprise of the popular characters from *What Price Glory?*, Sergeants Quirt and Flagg, now located in Brooklyn. Flagg is a Marine recruiting sergeant and Quirt runs a Turkish bath, but the action somehow takes them to Sweden and Turkey. Bogart's role as a marine was little more than a walk-on, and was cut from the final print.

A Holy Terror (1931)

Bogart's final film at Fox confirmed his disillusion with Hollywood and sent him scurrying back to New York. He was cast against the cowboy star George O'Brien, who flies west to seek his father's killer and crashes his plane into the ranch while Sally Eilers is performing her ablutions. Bogart plays the ranch foreman in love with her, and his nose is severely out of joint when she falls for the exciting millionaire.

Love Affair (1932)

Back in Hollywood after a brief appearance in *After All* on Broadway, Bogart was the male lead opposite Dorothy Mackaill, a popular young star of the 1920s nearing the end of her career. She plays an heiress and he a poor aeronautical engineer anxious to get backing for a new engine he has designed, and he teaches her to fly. They fall in love, she loses her fortune, and tries to marry a wealthy broker so that he can have his funding, a plan that goes adrift. There is far too much story for so short a film, but Bogart handles his role creditably, including a life-saving race against time as the dramatic climax.

Big City Blues (1932)

In this modest comedy-melodrama a hick from Indiana, played by Eric Linden, loose in New York, is fair game for spongers, con artists, and idlers. A party in his hotel room gets out of hand and a girl is murdered. Bogart, tenth-billed, has only a minor role, as one of a number of rowdy party guests, but the chippiness of his style is already making an impact. Memorable is the moment when he floors another over-enthusiastic partygoer (Lyle Talbot) with a powerful punch.

Three On a Match (1932)

Impressed by Bogart's appearance in *Midnight* (which had already been filmed although it was not released until two years later), Mervyn LeRoy cast him in his first real hoodlum part in this swift-moving account of three girls who reunite after their schooldays. One of them, Blondell, has been in reform school, and blackmail looms. Bogart plays a kidnapper hired by Lyle Talbot to abduct Davis's child. The pace is too fast to allow much of the plot to register. The title derives from a World War I superstition that lighting three cigarettes on the same match gave time for an enemy sniper to draw a bead.

Midnight (1934)

This embarrassingly poor film, based on a Broadway play, was shot in New York, enabling Bogart to take a break from the stage to play another gangster. The plot concerns a zealous jury foreman whose obduracy leads to a woman accused of a crime of passion going to the electric chair. The irony is that he then learns his own daughter has shot and killed her boyfriend after discovering his cheating. The victim is Bogart. Little attempt is to made to open up the original play, and the dialogue creaks unrealistically. After Bogart became a star it was reissued under the title *Call It Murder* with Bogart's billing position drastically amended.

Sidney Fox, Bogart, Bette Davis, Conrad Nagel
in *Bad Sister*.

Dorothy Mackaill and Humphrey Bogart, *Love Affair*.

The Petrified Forest (1936)

Leslie Howard and Humphrey Bogart had triumphed at the Broadhurst Theatre in Robert Sherwood's play set in the Black Mesa Bar-B-Q, a filling station and diner on a lonely Arizona highway. The quintessential English actor (whose roots were actually Hungarian) played Alan Squier, an intellectual backpacker who has turned his back on his pampered old life to roam the wilderness, brooding on the emptiness of civilization. Bogart was Duke Mantee, a murderous gangster who has escaped from the penitentiary and is the object of a manhunt across several states. Their paths meet in the humble desert service stop where their destinies are fulfilled. The play still had packed audiences when it closed because Howard wanted a vacation in Britain, and plans were then advanced to turn it into a film. Peggy Conklin, as the daughter of the establishment's owner who yearns to return to her birthplace in France, and falls in love with the Englishman, had her hopes dashed when Bette Davis was announced to play the role. Then Bogart, who had understood that he would play Duke, read in the trade press that Warner Bros. had cast Edward G. Robinson, Hollywood's most compelling portrayer of gangsters. However Howard, who controlled the film rights, cabled that without Bogart he would not sign a deal. During the run of the play the two contrasting actors had worked well together and their combination of world-weary esthete and ruthless mobster excited audiences, so Howard's subsequent attitude combined friendly loyalty with a shrewd perception of the importance of that relationship in box-office appeal. In effect he handed Bogart, now thirty-five, the first big-screen break after years of frustration.

However riveting *The Petrified Forest* was on stage it translated unsatisfactorily to film. A setting in the Arizona desert should have provided vivid images of wide-open spaces, but everything was shot on a Burbank sound stage, with saguaro cacti and empty sky painted on a backcloth. Little attempt is made to escape the proscenium arch, and characters make contrived entrances and embark on lengthy theatrical speeches. As the critic Pauline Kael remarked, the director Archie Mayo "gives you the feeling he has even retained the stage blocking." To rub in the staginess, the final shootout with the police goes unseen and is merely overheard from within the diner.

Sherwood's play is less of a thriller in which a group of people is holed up by a killer and his gang and made hostage, and more a social comment on the global malaise of the 1930s, a pessimistic statement on a world gone to the dogs. Squier finds himself drawn to the evil Mantee because he has had the guts to reject and attack entrenched values, and he makes a pact with him to take his life so that he can turn over a valuable life policy to the girl who loves him, enabling her to fulfill her dream. It now seems very dated, but more on account of the style than the content. There are occasional flashes of enlightenment, For instance, daringly for a film of its time, it makes a comment on racial oppression when the black member of Mantee's gang mocks the groveling subservience of a tycoon's black chauffeur.

In spite of its unusual literacy and a budgetary over-run that inflamed the producer Hal Wallis, who could not understand how a film with only one set could cost so much, *The Petrified Forest* was a hit with both critics and public, and while Howard was the star, the performances of Davis and Bogart drew much attention, altering their status within the industry for ever.

"I spend most of my time since I grew up in jail. And it looks like I spend the rest of my life dead." Bogart as Duke Mantee in *The Petrified Forest*

Previous Pages: Bogart, Mackaill, *Love Affair*.

Bogart as Duke Mantee at bay, *The Petrified Forest*.

Bullets or Ballots (1936)

Bogart, having edged Edward G. Robinson from *The Petrified Forest*, took a fourth-billed contract role in one of his vehicles, a typically fast-paced crime melodrama efficiently directed by William Keighley. Robinson played a police detective thrown off the force for slugging the commissioner, and gaining the kudos to be recruited into a mobster's organization. Bogart plays one of its members, who never trusts the Robinson character, and his hunch proves correct when it turns out that he has infiltrated on behalf of the police. Bogart once again is typecast as a remorseless killer, and the final confrontational shootout is with Robinson.

Two Against the World (1936)

In this undistinguished remake of Mervyn LeRoy's 1931 *Five Star Final* Bogart fills the Edward G. Robinson role and Harry Hayden the part originally played by Boris Karloff. The setting has changed from a muck-raking newspaper to a radio station, and as is the usual way with remakes, it is not an improvement. The plot concerns the resistance of the station's manager (Bogart) to the owner's plan to dramatize a twenty-year-old murder case, even though the perpetrator (Helen MacKellar) has paid her dues and is leading a respectable and anonymous life. The airings drive her and her husband to suicide and Bogart crusades against his employer to clean up broadcasting.

"The cold-blooded killer of 'The Petrified Forest' finds a new way to kill!"

Poster line for *Two Against the World*

China Clipper (1936)

Lindbergh fervor still prevailed in America nearly a decade after his epoch-making solo flight across the Atlantic. Pat O'Brien is the owner of a small airline who, inspired by Lindbergh, attempts to open up a Pacific route by backing a new aircraft on a record-breaking flight, with considerable sacrifice to personal and professional life. Bogart, once again downgraded to a subordinate role, plays a tough wise-cracking pilot, one of his old wartime buddies, and to give the character slightly more depth he has been made a widower. The end result is top-heavy and colorless, although for a moment the film's shortcomings are redeemed by a fine aerial shot of a clipper sliding through the air over the uncompleted Golden Gate Bridge.

Isle of Fury (1936)

Bogart was given a thin mustache to play the part of a fugitive from justice who has holed up on a remote Pacific island, where he has married and earns a living as a pearl trader. He rescues a lawman on his trail who eventually gives up, having seen that his quarry has reformed and is leading a blameless life. A remake of a three-year-old film, *The Narrow Corner*, it is disappointingly inept, and among its failings is an unconvincing tussle with an octopus, described as the most unconvincing monster in film history. For Bogart, who later alleged that he could not even remember making the film, the consolation was that it introduced him to the Californian island of Catalina, which would become one of his favorite haunts as a yachtsman.

Bogart, Barton MacLane, Edward G. Robinson, *Bullets or Ballots*.

Bogart, Pat O'Brien in *China Clipper*.

Black Legion (1937)

During the 1930s Warner made a number of social realist films, examining domestic malaises that shamed America's conscience. A brave approach, given that much of the audience would have been subscribers to the unworthy causes that came under fire. At the root of *Black Legion* was xenophobia, with Bogart cast as a disgruntled automobile factory worker passed over for promotion to a foreman's job in favor of a Polish immigrant. He joins a hooded secret order modeled after the Ku Klux Klan who in the name of patriotism launch vigilante attacks on foreigners perceived to be stealing American jobs. Reluctantly he takes part in a bizarre initiation ceremony, before being sucked into the zeal of the movement. Revenge is wreaked on the Pole, but Bogart loses his marriage and his job, and is tried for murder after shooting his best friend. In court he spurns mitigating factors and reveals the members of the organization even though it will lead to life imprisonment. The film was inspired by a real-life case in Michigan that had achieved headlines, but disappoints in that its thesis suggests that the xenophobic legionnaires are actually being exploited by ruthless businessmen pursuing their own agenda, which seems a cowardly copout from the reality. The producer Hal Wallis received threats during the production, and ran the risk of incurring opprobrium in some areas where sentiments condemned in the film were held to be valid. He also ran the risk of libel suits as some of the participants in Legion affairs had been elected to public office in militant districts. For Bogart it was an opportunity to act at last in a worthwhile movie, and he seized the chance, earning considerable critical approval. One critic, perhaps overstepping the mark, suggested that Bogart had it in him to be a contender for the coveted role of Rhett Butler in *Gone With the Wind*.

The Great O'Malley (1937)

Bogart's second film with Pat O'Brien is a capably directed melodrama with tearjerker elements. Bogart plays John Phillips, an unemployed man on his way to secure a job and is stopped by an over-zealous cop who tickets him for driving a decrepit car with a defective muffler. O'Malley, the policeman, played by O'Brien, has a reputation for his pettifogging adherence to the letter of the law. Phillips, having lost his chance for work thanks to the delay goes home to his wife and crippled daughter. Later, attempting to hock his war medals he has a violent argument with the pawnbroker and robs his till. O'Malley arrests him. The child is involved in an accident at his crossing, and having discovered that she is the daughter of a man in custody because of him he tends her and arranges an operation to fix her leg, as well as parole for her father. Phillips, unaware of the kindness, takes the opportunity on his release to shoot his perceived persecutor. Can it all end happily? Even given the stern "crime doesn't pay" strictures of the Hays Office, ways could be found to achieve an audience-pleasing result.

Marked Woman (1937)

Another Warner drama based on real events casts Bogart as a high-minded assistant district attorney anxious to secure the conviction of a prominent crime chief (Eduardo Ciannelli), who uses his nightclub as a front for prostitution (although in accordance with the strict production code that word is never heard, and the girls are described as "hostesses," a euphemism that would have fooled no-one). It is really Bette Davis's film, her first on her return to the studio following her sensation legal action in London, when she failed to be released from her contract. The girls are reluctant to give evidence against their boss, but when Davis's younger sister, played by Jane Bryan, is killed, she talks, suffering a violent attack that leaves her facially scarred. The screenplay does not give enough depth to Bogart, on the right side of the law, and he seems less colorful than usual. His character is modeled on Thomas E. Dewey, a crusading attorney who later ran for president, and Ciannelli's vice king is unmistakably meant to be the gangster "Lucky" Luciano.

Kid Galahad (1937)

Bogart, in his element again, plays a crooked boxing promoter with chilling relish, capable of bringing silence to a crowded room as soon as he enters it. A manager, Edward G. Robinson grooms a bellhop (Wayne Morris) who has been humiliated by Bogart, into a heavyweight championship contender against Bogart's man. Robinson almost has the big fight thrown because Morris has fallen for his sister (Jane Bryan) but Bette Davis as his mistress intercedes causing him to change his mind, leading to an eventual bloody shootout. The joint casting of Robinson and Bogart went down well at the box-office and Curtiz's confident direction delivered a crisp, taut, energy-filled melodrama.

San Quentin (1937)

A formulaic prison movie, *San Quentin* may well have seemed fresher on first release because so many films since have taken their cue from it. Pat O'Brien, as the new captain of the yard, tries to reverse the oppressive regime of his predecessor, Barton MacLane. The former captain gets his revenge by suggesting to Bogart, a troublesome prisoner who O'Brien has helped to straighten out, that far from being a benefactor his usurper has designs on his sister (Ann Sheridan). After a prison break Bogart makes his way to her apartment intending to shoot O'Brien, but she pleads that she really loves him, bringing about a change of heart.

Bette Davis, Humphrey Bogart in *Marked Woman*.

Dead End (1937)

A Broadway hit, *Dead End* was transferred to the screen by Sam Goldwyn who decided that, rather than let the director William Wyler shoot this New York story on location, he would confine it to a Hollywood sound stage, creating an elaborate set that would capture the cheek-by-jowl proximity of plush East Side apartments inhabited by the rich to the squalid dockside tenements of the poor. Bogart plays a gangster with a heavy murder record who revisits the slums of his upbringing, and is idolized by the neighborhood kids. It is the first screen appearance of the Dead End Kids (who later were known as the Bowery Boys and would go on to become staples of the B picture). At the opposite end of the spectrum is Joel McCrea as an idealistic architect who dreams of tearing the squalor apart and who eventually proves to be the gangster's nemesis. The perfectionist craftsmanship of Wyler, always an actor's director, gives the film considerable power, and was a triumph for Bogart in the first of several parts that would have gone to the more starry George Raft, had he not been so hesitant.

Stand-In (1937)

Bogart's second film with Leslie Howard is an engaging lampoon of Hollywood. Colossal Pictures is about to be sold to an asset stripper whose plan is to close the studio, and Howard is empowered by the New York owners to take charge, curb the extravagance and make it viable again. Knowing nothing about films, not even knowing who Shirley Temple and Clark Gable are, he is expected by the predators to be an easy pushover, but with Joan Blondell as his eager and protective Girl Friday and Bogart as a gifted, underestimated filmmaker driven by frustration to drink, he surprises everyone. Jack Carson plays an odious Hollywood PR man who seems like the same character in George Cukor's *A Star is Born* seventeen years later. The satire is sharp, but takes a tediously dated turn when trite capital-versus-labor arguments are clumsily dragged in. Bogart, determinedly un-gangsterish for once, wears open-neck shirts and strolls around with a Scots terrier under his arm.

Swing Your Lady (1938)

Bogart starring in a hillbilly musical? It happened, although it was an episode he preferred to forget. Rustic humor was in vogue following Paramount's *Mountain Music* and it was a transparent attempt by another studio to cash in. Bogart plays a wrestling promoter who turns up in the Ozarks with the mountainous Nat Pendleton, and matches him against the local woman blacksmith (Louise Fazenda). The Weaver Brothers and Elviry supply much of the music and would later turn up in a string of low-budget films, while Penny Singleton, the leading lady would become forever remembered for playing the eternal comic-strip housewife, Blondie, in a long-running series. Also in the cast as a reporter was Ronald Reagan. None of this was to stop the film from disaster at the box-office.

Crime School (1938)

Bogart was reunited with the Dead End Kids—but in this melodrama he is on the right side of the law as a commissioner who takes over a boys' institution on finding that it is being administered by a corrupt sadist. He introduces an honor system, which comes under fire when the kids escape. The deposed superintendent has manipulated them by alleging Bogart has evil designs on the sister of a boy who has been ill-treated. It is an unexceptional film, following a path already well-trodden by *San Quentin* and James Cagney's 1933 picture *The Mayor of Hell*.

Men Are Such Fools (1938)

Not many films fashion a title from their last line, which here is the summing-up comment uttered by Priscilla Lane, who has been involved in a love triangle with Wayne Morris and Bogart. She works in an advertising agency and places career advancement more highly than marital contentment, a most unfashionable stance in the 1930s. Bogart is the agency hotshot who tries to usurp Morris and uncharacteristically is knocked to the ground in their final confrontation. Busby Berkeley was famous for his extravagantly choreographed musicals, but here he is in the wrong element. *The New York Times*, commenting on what the film was about, said "about an hour too long."

Previous Pages: Gregg Toland shoots, William Wyler directs Joel McCrea, Allen Jenkins, Bogart in *Dead End*.

Priscilla Lane, Bogart in *Men Are Such Fools*.

Racket Busters (1938)

An efficiently directed programmer sees Bogart back in the familiar public-enemy role in which he tries to control the food supply by taking over the trucking business. His efforts to force drivers to join his protection organization are fiercely opposed by George Brent, who is viciously intimidated to prevent him from testifying. Walter Abel is the special prosecutor who finally breaks Bogart's hold. The character is modeled on Thomas E. Dewey, whose crime-busting exploits inspired several Hollywood movies.

The Amazing Dr. Clitterhouse (1938)

An amusing theater piece in which a criminal psychologist, on Broadway played by Cedric Hardwicke but here by Edward G. Robinson, bases his new book on practical experience, and actually becomes a jewel thief to test his theories. Claire Trevor plays a fence with Bogart organizing a gang of thieves on her behalf, but the doctor's presence diminishes his leadership. When the last heist is over and Robinson has returned to respectability Bogart traces him and starts blackmailing. Robinson decides to try out the psychology of a murderer, which leads to curtains for Bogart and an extremely interesting trial. One of the screenwriters who adapted Barré Lyndon's play was John Huston, the first time his screen credit appeared on a Bogart film.

Angels With Dirty Faces (1938)

It is James Cagney's film, c   of his best, as he returns to a New York slum neighborhood in which he grew up, having become a flashy underworld hero to the l   al youth (the Dead End Kids again). His childhood best friend, Pat O'Brien, has turned in another direction and is the respected parish priest. Bogart does not have much to do, but is excellent as Cagney's lawyer, who becomes a nightclub owner and double-crosses him. Cagney guns him down as he grovels for his life. Tried and sentenced, the hoodlum is cocky and defiant until the last, when O'Brien makes a personal plea for him to go to the chair not with his head high but as a sniveling coward, so that the kids will not elevate h   martyrdom. He does so, but no one will know if he is obliging an old friend or if it is for real, and the cold-blooded killer was genuine   ily livered.

"Why can't the best actor in the world play anything but heavies?"

Mayo Methot

Bogart, Edward G. Robinson in
The Amazing Dr. Clitterhouse.

Following Pages: Bogart, Cagney, *Angels With Dirty Faces.*

King of the Underworld (1939)

A loose remake of the 1935 Paul Muni film *Dr. Socrates* casts Kay Francis in the role of a doctor compromised by a gangster with a Napoleonic complex, almost destroying her career, but who later outwits him together with his gang by temporarily blinding them with eyedrops, and handing them over to justice. It fails through implausibility of plot, aimless direction, and over-acting, with Bogart as guilty as others for stretching the material. It was, however, the first film in which he was given star billing, with Francis, a former box-office heavyweight, relegated below the title and on her way out, but receiving a substantially higher salary than him.

The Oklahoma Kid (1939)

The Cherokee Strip in 1893 finds homesteaders confronted by callous outlaws who brutally resist their attempts to settle. Neither James Cagney nor Bogart are comfortable in this western. It is as if they have been unhappily transplanted from the mean streets to the unfamiliar wide open spaces. Both are badmen, although Cagney as the Kid has redeeming features. Bogart, clad head-to-foot in black, a king of gambling and lawlessness, is as ruthless as any sagebrush villain, and he and Cagney have the inevitable showdown. It is reasonably entertaining, with many of the familiar trappings of westerns, but remains curiously unsatisfying on account of the unsettling displacement of the two stars.

"You take care of their virtues, I'll take care of their vices. Simple, ain't it?"

Bogart as Whip McCord in *The Oklahoma Kid*

You Can't Get Away With Murder (1939)

Yet another prison drama, with Bogart once again as a cold-hearted crook, this time forcing his young accomplice (Billy Halop) in a pawnshop robbery to keep quiet after he kills the owner and an innocent man is convicted of his crime. Both wind up in Sing Sing on another charge, and, in order to ensure his silence, Bogart shoots Halop under cover of a breakout. The title says it all. Bogart has left it too late and goes to the chair. There is a perfunctory, well-oiled feel to the proceedings.

Dark Victory (1939)

One of Bette Davis's most cherished performances is Judith Traherne, a pampered, hugely wealthy young socialite who cares for horses, partying and shopping, but keeps getting these headaches. A personable brain surgeon (George Brent) suspects and then confirms that she has only months to live. He swears not to tell her but she finds out anyway and they have a brief, idyllic marriage leading to a celebrated lachrymose fadeout. Bogart is an Irish horse trainer who runs her stables, has a thing about her that is partly shared and which might have sent the film in a more interesting direction. He is good, but again miscast and his version of an Irish accent is about as plausible as Dick Van Dyke's cockney. Another ending in which he posthumously wins the Grand National for her was scrapped after bad reactions from preview audiences.

Bette Davis, Bogart in *Dark Victory*.

The Roaring Twenties (1939)

James Cagney, adept as he was at playing underworld characters, made Eddie Bartlett one of the best, then had a ten-year hiatus before portraying Cody Jarrett in *White Heat*. In any case Warner were coming to the glorious end of their 1930s gangster cycle. Here Cagney, Bogart, and Jeffrey Lynn are trench buddies in World War I. The latter goes into law but the other two make the most of Prohibition, setting up as rival bootleg bosses. Cagney's empire collapses with the stock-market crash in 1929, and he is reduced to driving a cab for a living, but Bogart prospers. The melodramatic shootout is unforgettable. He seeks out Bogart, the top dog, and shoots him but the gang returns fire, and he collapses, mortally wounded, on the snow-covered steps of a church. A patrolman asks Gladys George who he was. She says: "He used to be a big shot."

"I always say, when you got a job to do, get somebody else to do it."

Bogart as George Hally in *The Roaring Twenties*

The Return of Dr. X (1939)

In a role that seemed more suitable for Boris Karloff, Bogart is an executed killer who has been brought back to life by a fellow doctor, played by John Litel, but can only survive on a regular intake of blood. Rosemary Lane almost becomes one of his victims. Bogart's appearance is startling, pallid, and bespectacled, with a wide streak of white coursing through his black hair. During his Warner years he endured many bizarre strokes of casting, but none weirder than this.

Invisible Stripes (1939)

George Raft and Bogart rivaled each other as Warner's tough guys, but here teamed together it is obvious that the latter is a superior actor. They play newly released convicts. Raft tries to follow the harder option of going straight while Bogart returns to his interrupted crime career. Raft is reluctantly drawn back as well, but is determined that his younger brother (William Holden) does not tread the same path. The outcome is predictable.

"You think changin' your uniform means anything, you'll still be wearin' stripes. You may not be able to see 'em, but they'll be there all right."

Bogart to Raft on the ex-convict ethos in *Invisible Stripes*

Frank McHugh with Cagney and Bogart
in *The Roaring Twenties*.

1940–1949

George Raft turned down *High Sierra*, unwilling to play an over-the-hill gangster. Other Warner heavies, including Cagney, Robinson, and Muni also passed. At the end of the line was Bogart, who had to yield top billing to Ida Lupino. The authority of his performance as Roy "Mad Dog" Earle ensured that would never happen again. From then on he was always number one. The pot-boiling semi-remake of *Kid Galahad*, *The Wagons Roll at Night* was already in the works, but it was followed by the most important watershed in Bogart's career development. Again Raft demurred and to Bogart's benefit, this time because he did not wish to be in the hands of a directing tyro. As it was John Huston it seemed a strange error of judgment, and *The Maltese Falcon* established the iconic image of the trench-coated, hunch-shouldered figure of Bogart, the front brim of his gray fedora tilted downward to suggest his melancholy impatience with a flawed world. Not only is film noir defined, but also the quintessence of the private eye: hard-boiled, cynical, ruthless, courageous, driven by an ethical code that he alone understands and respects.

It paved the way to the elevation of Bogart as the greatest romantic hero of World War II in what unexpectedly turned out to be its most popular film. Hollywood at its Hollywoodest, *Casablanca* is about the realization of the impossibility of disengagement. Rick renounces Ilsa because that tiny gesture will help make the world a better place. His sacrifice made sense to millions whose lives had been shattered by war. The intent still remains powerful, but in the context of wartime it must have been overwhelming.

Serendipitous in retrospect, the production at the time was grueling. Great care had to be taken to photograph Ingrid Bergman and Bogart so that she was not seen to tower over him. Mayo unjustly suspected them of an affair, and on several occasions descended on set making jealous outbursts. The director Michael Curtiz did nothing to dispel his reputation for being a hard taskmaster. Months after the release the Bogarts departed on a morale-raising trip to Europe and Africa, including the real Casablanca, to entertain service personnel. In Italy their noisy brawling upset a general's slumber and he truncated their tour.

Bogart made other war films, such as *Action in the North Atlantic*, *Sahara*, and *Passage to Marseille*, but none was exceptional. While making the latter Howard Hawks visited the set and introduced him to a nineteen-year-old *Harper's Bazaar* model from New York who had been to acting school. Hawks had given her a contract. Lauren Bacall was stunning and however nervous inwardly she projected cool self-assurance. Cast together in an adaption of Ernest Hemingway's *To Have and Have Not*, a sort of waterborne re-run of *Casablanca* set in the West Indies island of Martinique, they obliged the director by falling in love, emitting an on-screen chemistry that completely overcame her lack of screen-acting experience. Mayo's

Claude Rains, Paul Henreid, Ingrid Bergman,
Humphrey Bogart, *Casablanca*.

time was up. He now had three marital failures, a fact that did not sit well with Lauren's mother who, was also concerned by his advanced middle-age and the fact that he was not Jewish.

After *The Big Sleep*, a noir masterwork, they married, on May 21, 1945, at the novelist Louis Bromfield's Ohio farm. For Bogart it was a case of fourth time lucky. He had acquired a wife who was young, beautiful, talented, witty, spirited, devoted, who would give him two children and contentedly see out his days. They only made two more films together, the odd thriller *Dark Passage* and the much more satisfactory Huston-directed *Key Largo*. She was adrift when cast without him in *Confidential Agent*. He was resentful when obliged to perform with an inferior Bacall-look-alike, Lizabeth Scott in *Dead Reckoning*. In the meantime his lifestyle had changed drastically. The *Sluggy* had gone, replaced by a trim 55-foot yacht, the *Santana*, which after Lauren became the love of his life. Warner had given him a generous new contract placing him at last in the highest-paid echelon of stars.

Bogart was privately appalled by the questionable actions of the House Un-American Activities Committee, which was driving many directors, writers, and actors out of the business if they had any present or past communist connections. He, Bacall and other Hollywood luminaries, including Danny Kaye, Gene Kelly, and John Huston, took part in a protest in Washington. Politically he was mildly left-leaning, had been a supporter of Roosevelt, and would champion Adlai Stevenson. He was, however, shocked that most of the so-called Hollywood Ten, who he felt might have escaped persecution had they pleaded the First Amendment, exercised their testimony to make propaganda, and feeling that he had been used, he withdrew from the arena, regretting his actions. In retrospect it was a wise move as far as his career was concerned. The press had already become critical, and his much-hated boss Jack Warner was a particularly savage Red baiter. It was a shameful period in Hollywood history.

Huston had provided Bogart with another of his best parts, that of the gold-hungry down-and-out Fred C. Dobbs, who embarks on the Mexican quest for *The Treasure of the Sierra Madre*. Bogart also formed his own production company, Santana, to develop the kind of films he felt would not get made inside the studio system. Relations with Warner ebbed away, and Santana films were released mostly though Columbia. In the best of the handful that were made, *In a Lonely Place*, directed by Nicholas Ray, he plays Dixon Steele, a jaded screenwriter, an intelligent man ground down by that system, who becomes involved in the death of a girl. Bogart, a literate, well-read man, often sought out the company of writers as his watering-hole companions, and his portrayal bore the mark of keen observation.

Virginia City (1940)

The closing moments of *Dodge City* suggest that *Virginia City* will be the sequel, but sadly it is not. The character's names have changed and Olivia De Havilland has been replaced as Errol Flynn's romantic interest by the much less appealing Miriam Hopkins. The time is the Civil War, with Errol Flynn, a Union officer endeavoring to stop Randolph Scott hijacking a gigantic gold shipment to boost the Confederacy's declining cause. Bogart plays a Mexican half-breed bandit hired by Scott as part of the plan, but unable to resist the temptation of grabbing the gold for himself—a fatal error. Bogart sports a narrow mustache, speaks with a cartoon accent, and is clearly ill at ease.

It All Came True (1940)

In this engaging whimsical curiosity Bogart is an on-the-run murderer who goes to cover in one of those theatrical boarding houses that only exist in movies. Taking an interest in the residents, who are either forgotten or unemployed, he encourages them to open a Gay Nineties nightclub on the premises, giving them all a purpose in life, but his altruism not surprisingly attracts the notice of the police. It is one of the few roles rejected by George Raft that might have been better left untouched.

Brother Orchid (1940)

In this unusual dramatic comedy a mobster (Edward G. Robinson) is forced out by Bogart. Finding the going too tough he embarks on a new way of life by entering a monastery, where the brothers welcome him. He becomes an expert horticulturalist, cultivating flowers which are sold to help the poor. Then Bogart's gang wrecks the market by extorting protection money from the flower sellers. Robinson returns briefly to the world outside to deal forcefully with the racketeer, returning to carry on as "Brother Orchid."

They Drive By Night (1940)

The structure of this film seems broken-backed for good reason, with the first part a gripping action thriller in which two brothers (George Raft, Bogart) run their own small trucking business in the face of pressure to make their payments and stave off heavy competition. Bogart loses an arm in a crash, and Raft is forced to join a big fleet. The owner's wife, Ida Lupino, is infatuated with him, and murders her husband (Alan Hale). However, Raft is in love with a former truckstop waitress (Ann Sheridan) and Lupino, enraged, pins the killing on him. The first part of the film is from a novel, but the rest, including a tense courtroom sequence, derives from *Bordertown*, a 1935 Bette Davis vehicle, completely altering the mood established earlier.

"*Virginia City* proves that no play or film in which Bogart wore a mustache was any good."

Jeffrey Meyers, Bogart: A Life in Hollywood

Ida Lupino and Bogart in *They Drive by Night*.

High Sierra (1941)

After more than a decade in the movies Bogart was seen as one of the most dependable performers on the Warner lot, a worthy member of the select band of tough guys, which included Edward G. Robinson, James Cagney, and George Raft. However, he was a junior to them, often playing second string in their "A" features. Raft was unduly selective over the parts he was offered and on several occasions Bogart benefited from his hesitations and refusals. The role of Roy "Mad Dog" Earle was one of them, and Paul Muni had also been actively in the running but dropped out after a contract row. The big decision was taken to make Bogart the star and it became a significant landmark in his career. Even though Ida Lupino is first-billed, the combined contribution of Raoul Walsh's pacy, energetic direction and a screenplay co-written by John Huston allows Bogart to deliver a nuanced, subtle characterization with sensitivities not expected of a dangerous criminal.

Roy Earle is a hangover from the earlier, more lawless Prohibition era, and is released on parole after spending many years in the penitentiary. He has been set up by a dying crime baron to lead the one last heist that will give him a retirement pension of sorts. His handicap is the poor caliber of his appointed associates who do not have the ruthless dedication of hoodlums in the old days. The robbery goes wrong, a watchman is killed, two of the gang die in a car crash and the jewels are too hot to fence. Earle has also been sidetracked by an infatuation for a lame teenager he has met on the highway as she journeys with her migrating grandparents to a better life in California. He pays for an operation to cure her condition, but she then turns into a suburban brat with no interest in him. Ida Lupino, however, playing the female member of the gang whose presence he has previously opposed, becomes his lover during the difficult post-robbery days. After a failed hold-up to replenish his empty pockets he takes to the mountains in a desperate bid to flee the state, but is cornered high above the timberline, and picked off by a police sniper.

There is far more location shooting than was common in films of the period, giving it a heightened sense of reality, and impressive use is made of the Sierra Nevada landscape. Walsh also copes well with potentially awkward encumbrances that detract from the impetus of the story, the subplot with the handicapped girl for instance, and the presence of a faithful dog who unwittingly leads the pursuers to their quarry. Bogart transcends all such near-maudlin shortcomings by the power of his performance. His appearance, with his prison pallor and a horrible haircut, shorn sides surmounted by a graying mat, perfectly suggests a man whose only experience outdoors for many years has been the penal yard. From now on there would be no occasions when Bogart was not given top billing.

"Sometimes I feel I don't know what it's all about any more."

Bogart as Roy "Mad Dog" Earle in *High Sierra*

The Wagons Roll at Night (1941)

There was an awkward interim after *High Sierra* in which contract rows stymied Bogart's advancement. He received top billing in *The Wagons Roll at Night*, a reworking of the *Kid Galahad* story with the boxer replaced by a circus lion-tamer (Eddie Albert). Bogart, the owner of the traveling carnival, is obsessed with his young sister (Joan Leslie) and takes it badly when the tamer falls for her. He plans to send him into the cage of a mad killer lion, but the fortune-teller (Sylvia Sidney), who is his girlfriend, persuades him otherwise. The concluding tragedy turns out to be his, not the young lovers'. It is pale stuff after *High Sierra* but happily would be followed by much greater glory.

Bogart in *High Sierra*.

The Maltese Falcon (1941)

Were it necessary to name only one work as the epitome of film noir this surely would have to be it. The first film to be directed by John Huston, hitherto known only as a writer, it defines the genre. The familiar ingredients are all there: The shadowy cinematography, the nocturnal mean streets, the array of bizarre, self-interested characters, the inevitable *femme fatale*, and at its heart the hard-boiled hero whose morals may not be too good, yet at pains to uphold a principle: "When a man's partner is killed, he's supposed to do something about it. It doesn't make any difference what you thought of him. He was your partner and you're supposed to do something about it." This noble attitude is tempered by his assertion that the death is bad for business and his swift termination of an affair with his partner's wife.

Bogart, once again taking a rejected George Raft role (it is said that he was unprepared to trust a neophyte director), fitted the role of San Francisco private detective Sam Spade as though it had been written for him. The belted trench coat and the soft-brimmed fedora became a Bogart trademark. It is perhaps a surprise that this great milestone film is not merely a remake, but a remake of a remake. Its two predecessors have justly been forgotten, confounding the commonly accepted movie wisdom that no rehash is ever as good as the original.

Huston's approach was uncharacteristic. Like Hitchcock and Welles he storyboarded his screenplay, and with Arthur Edeson, his director of photography, he devised flowing camera movements that drove the plot along, yet were so subtle that the audience would hardly have been aware. At the time some of the techniques were innovative, and even today although much has been subsequently imitated, there is still a sense of freshness.

The plot is so convoluted it is almost meaningless, and in the end hardly matters. It is a classic instance of Hitchcock's famous McGuffin theory in action, in which a vaguely defined plot device impels the narrative, in this case a wild-goose chase. Or rather, a quest for another kind of bird, a fabulous ancient statuette filled with priceless treasure, but the search hardly strays far from Spade's shabby walk-up office. A mysterious attractive woman (Mary Astor), who quickly offers three different names, is the first of a picaresque band of greedy figures who cross Spade's threshold. Spade's partner, Miles Archer (Jerome Cowan) is found shot. Peter Lorre floats in as the epicene Joel Cairo, Sidney Greenstreet, in a stunning debut at sixty-one, is the genial fat man Casper Guttman, and Elisha Cook Jr. plays Wilmer, the inept bodyguard dismissed by Spade as a "gunsel," the censors unaware that it was nothing to do with being a gunman, but a Yiddish vulgarity for a young homosexual. The yarn is meant to be a whodunnit, although for many years a bronze plaque near the street corner of Bush and Stockton in San Francisco where Miles Archer met his doom, gives it away. In any case the denouement in which Brigid O'Shaugnessy (Astor) is unmasked by the smitten Spade ("I won't play the sap for you") who hands her into custody saying: "I hope they don't hang you, precious, by that sweet neck" and adding that if she gets off he will be waiting. Twenty years is a long time and her bloom will have faded, so she should not keep her hopes up. The apposite last line, a Shakespearean reference, was supplied by Bogart himself. When asked what the falcon actually is, he says: "The stuff that dreams are made of."

Bogart, Elisha Cook Jr. *The Maltese Falcon.* | Bogart as Sam Spade, *The Maltese Falcon.*

All Through the Night (1942)

Pearl Harbor and America's entry into World War II occurred six weeks before the film's release, which may have been bad timing because events had become too serious to treat the Fifth Column espionage threat as a butt for Runyonesque jokes. Bogart plays Gloves Donahue, a former gangster who earns his living from gambling, but when faced with Nazi agents he discovers patriotism matters. A girl refugee is kidnapped by a spy ring that is holding her father hostage. Gloves and his old criminal gang go after them and thwart a plan to blow up a battleship in New York harbor. It is fast-paced, entertaining, filled with a top-line cast of seasoned character actors, and no doubt greatly aided war morale.

The Big Shot (1942)

There is nothing new about this melodrama and it could easily have been made in the pre-*Maltese Falcon* era. In a promising first part Bogart plays a three-time loser, a convicted former big shot who will go down for life for his next crime. He is cajoled into committing a robbery but is forced off it at the last moment by his girlfriend (Irene Manning), wife of a criminal lawyer. Nevertheless, a witness falsely identifies him and he is sent to the penitentiary, but escapes, killing a guard, to make a *High Sierra*-style dash for the mountains. Before he dies from police gunfire he has had time to settle his accounts with those who betrayed him. Bogart's talent is largely wasted in unmemorable dross.

Across the Pacific (1942)

John Huston left the production for war service before shooting had finished, leaving an uncredited Vincent Sherman in charge. It may account for the bizarre exaggeration of the finale, in which Bogart seems to be taking on the Japanese army by himself as he thwarts their dastardly plan to seize the Panama Canal. The opening is much more solid and exciting as he is drummed out of the U.S. Army in disgrace by a court-martial, and despairingly sets sail for the Far East to find somewhere that will have him. En route he falls in with Sydney Greenstreet, a Japanese agent, but it turns out that Bogart is actually a U.S. infiltrator and the court-martial was a sham. It is a fairly shameless potboiler after *The Maltese Falcon* but Mary Astor returns as the mysterious heroine. The focal point of the Japanese attack was to have been Pearl Harbor, but reality caught up and hasty rewriting ensued.

Marty Callahan: It don't make no difference to me who runs the country, as long as they stay out of my way.

Gloves Donahue: That's just it, they're not going to stay out of your way.

Marty Callahan: Oh, yes, they will.

Gloves Donahue: Oh, now listen, big shot, they'll tell you what time you get up in the morning and what time you go to bed at night. They'll tell you what you eat, what kind of clothes you can wear, what you drink. They'll even tell you the morning paper you can read.

Marty Callahan: They can't do that, it's against the law!

Bogart as Gloves explains Nazism to Barton MacLane, *All Through the Night*

Previous Pages: Peter Lorre as Joel Cairo, Humphrey Bogart, *The Maltese Falcon*.

Bogart in convict uniform in *The Big Shot*.

130   Bogie

Casablanca (1942)

By now well into his forties, and stereotyped as a Hollywood tough guy, Bogart emerged as a consequence of the astonishing success of this film the most potent romantic hero of World War II. *Casablanca* won the Academy Award for the Best Picture of 1943 (it had opened in New York at the end of 1942, but not until early 1943 in Los Angeles, thus qualifying under the Academy's rules as a 1943 contender). The most popular American film made during the war had begun as a routine studio picture, based on a little-known play, a love triangle in exotic surroundings with an espionage background. Yet again George Raft turned down the lead, the part of Rick Blaine, a steadfastly neutral but tormented American who owns a nightclub in Casablanca, the Moroccan seaport that was then an uneasy outpost of Vichy France. His best friend is the smooth chief of police, Louis Renault (Claude Rains) who charms all sides to survive. Into the club one night comes Ilsa (Ingrid Bergman), his former lover in Paris who suddenly left him as the Germans invaded, and with her is Victor (Paul Henreid), the husband he knew nothing of, a hero of the resistance. The old passion reignites, and Rick's conscience consumes him. At the end he abandons his neutrality by shooting a senior Nazi (Conrad Veidt), giving cause for Louis to issue the immortal order: "Round up the usual suspects." He then makes Ilsa fly out with Victor, knowing she does not love her husband, but aware that he will have an important task to fulfill for the free world. Rick tells Ilsa: "The problems of three little people don't amount to a hill of beans in this crazy world."

How the film was to conclude was not decided until late in production, and unhappy endings were thought to be bad for the box-office. Nevertheless that was the direction in which it was decided the story had to go. One of the common experiences of wartime was separation and parting, and the doomed love of Rick and Ilsa seemed to have resonances that matched the feelings of the many who saw it.

It was a swiftly made, economical film, driven by the talented but dictatorial Michael Curtiz. The medina of Casablanca was fabricated on the backlot of the Warner studio at Burbank out of discarded sets from *The Desert Song*, and the only location was a brief airport scene. The cast, led by its Hungarian director, was largely from other countries, many of its members genuine refugees from the Nazis, and Bogart and Dooley Wilson, his faithful pianist who sings the haunting "As Time Goes By," were almost the only Americans in the film. Ingrid Bergman had been a big star in neutral Sweden and had resisted offers to appear in German cinema, preferring Hollywood. She and Bogart teamed well together, so much so that his wife, Mayo Methot, frequently assailed him with jealous rages when visiting the set. Nevertheless the statuesque Bergman's casting presented problems for the camera department, and care had to be taken to ensure that she did not appear to be towering over the slightly built Bogart.

Another factor that helped *Casblanca* to achieve its extraordinary success was that in November 1942, the same month as the New York opening, U.S. forces seized the city, and in January 1943 Churchill and Roosevelt conferred there, and the historic meeting determined a policy of unconditional surrender as the basis on which the rest of the war would be fought.

Rick: I'm saying it because it's true. Inside of us, we both know you belong with Victor. You're part of his work, the thing that keeps him going. If that plane leaves the ground and you're not with him, you'll regret it. Maybe not today. Maybe not tomorrow, but soon and for the rest of your life.

Ilsa: But what about us?

Rick: We'll always have Paris. We didn't have, we lost it until you came to Casablanca. We got it back last night.

Ilsa: When I said I would never leave you.

Rick: And you never will. But I've got a job to do, too. Where I'm going, you can't follow. What I've got to do, you can't be any part of. Ilsa, I'm no good at being noble, but it doesn't take much to see that the problems of three little people don't amount to a hill of beans in this crazy world. Someday you'll understand that. Now, now.... Here's looking at you kid.

The most famous movie farewell, Bogart and Bergman, *Casablanca*

Bogart (Rick) and Bergman (Ilsa), *Casablanca*.

Dooley Wilson as Sam at piano, Bogart in Rick's Café.   Bogart as Rick, Peter Lorre as Ugarte.

Three little people in a crazy world, Henreid, Bergman, Bogart.

Renault (Rains) orders "Round up the usual suspects".

Action in the North Atlantic (1943)

This tribute to the civilian Navy, the seamen who manned the convoys of merchant ships across the Atlantic, defying the ever-present danger of undersea attack by U-boat, has a high degree of spectacular action and personal courage, and an excusable infusion of propaganda for the Allied cause. Audiences in Britain would have been aware that very print of the film they were watching had reached them as a result of the bravery it portrays. Bogart is excellent as the easygoing first officer to the stolid skipper played by Raymond Massey, and prefers it that way, regarding a master's job as too onerous. That will change when Massey is badly wounded during a run to Murmansk. The crew is an array of different representative Americans, each with a chance to express their ethnic diversity and pride in nationhood, a common theme in wartime movies. Yet the screenwriter was denounced after the war by the House Un-American Activities Committee and favorable references to the Russians, then staunch Allies, were cited as evidence of his pro-communist leanings. Bogart adopts the new war-hero mode skillfully, but one instance of the old Bogie surfaces when during a barroom sojourn ashore he quietly slugs into unconsciousness an unpatriotic loudmouth who is disrupting the lady's song.

Thank Your Lucky Stars (1943)

Paramount and Warner led the studios in creating star-studded patriotic extravaganzas with flimsy storylines that generally indicated how Hollywood was handling the war effort. Here Bogart has a brief cameo in which his tough guy act impresses nobody. "Hey, I must be losing my touch."

Sahara (1943)

In this engaging war action-adventure Bogart plays an American sergeant in command of a tank cruising the desert after the fall of Tobruk. Historically he is perhaps rather too far east, and is in the territory of the British Eighth Army, but Hollywood knows its box-office. The quest for water becomes crucial, especially after he picks up a United Nations-worth of stragglers and prisoners. Using the resourcefulness of a professional soldier, he persuades the others to entice an armored column of water-depleted Germans to a dry well, and then take them. The story was adapted from a Russian film, the action switched from central Asia to North Africa, providing more ammunition for the HUAC witch-hunters to pillory the screenwriter, the wretched John Howard Lawson.

Passage to Marseille (1944)

It proved not to be enough in this instance to round up the "usual suspects" of *Casablanca*; Peter Lorre, Sydney Greenstreet, Claude Rains, together with Bogart and Michael Curtiz as director. The structure, often involving multiple flashbacks, militates against simple storytelling, and Bogart's character is not merely ambiguous, but contradictory, a mixture of fervent anti-fascism and ruthless cruelty. He plays an idealistic French journalist framed for murder who escapes from Devil's Island with a group of patriots, with whom he eventually joins to engage the enemy. Ridiculous subplots including the love interest with Michele Morgan, a shadow of the Bogart-Bergman passion in *Casablanca*, help to torpedo this convoluted, badly scripted and semi-coherent failure.

"Warner's finally got a name for you, it's great. Jose O'Toole. It's got all the right ethnic implications, and besides there a sort of lilt."

Bogart upsetting new actor Dane Clark with a bogus name change

Bogart, Raymond Massey in *Action in the North Atlantic*.

Previous Pages: Rick sends Ilsa out of his life at *Casablanca*'s end.

Bogart, Patrick O'Moore, *Sahara*.

To Have and Have Not (1944)

In Martinique after the fall of France Bogart plays an American fishing-boat skipper who wants to stay neutral, but agrees to smuggle an underground leader for much-needed money. The atmosphere is steamy and exotic, although it was filmed mostly on the Burbank studio lot, and the storyline makes the best of a minor Hemingway novel by ignoring most of it. What turned the film into a hit was the introduction on screen of Lauren Bacall, whose immediate rapport with Bogart ignited the proceedings, the force of her presence eclipsing her acting inexperience. She also generated the immortal "whistle" moment. "You know how to whistle, don't you Steve? You just put your lips together, and blow."

Conflict (1945)

Made in 1943, before *Passage to Marseille*, this thriller was stockpiled by Warner while they were reserving their priorities for topical war films. Bogart plays a wife murderer who conceals his crime by pretending to be immobilized with a broken leg. His false status as a widower enables him to develop a romantic interest in his sister-in-law (Alexis Smith), which is not reciprocated. A wily psychologist (Sydney Greenstreet) suspects him. Then strange things happen that suggest to him that his wife is not really dead, and has come back to torment him into insanity or confession. A strong cast ensures that *Conflict* is watchable, but generally it reeks of implausibility.

Two Guys from Milwaukee (1946)

Humphrey Bogart appears briefly in a cameo in this comedy in which a deposed Balkan prince becomes a Milwaukee beer salesman and achieves his dream of meeting Lauren Bacall.

Lauren Bacall, Bogart, *To Have and Have Not.*   The new team, Bogart and Bacall, *To Have and Have Not.*

The Big Sleep (1946)

Alongside Dashiell Hammett's San Francisco private detective, Sam Spade, Raymond Chandler's Philip Marlowe is an altogether more complex character, with sensitivities that would be alien to his more basic counterpart. His territory is the Los Angeles area and he is just as likely to find lowlifes and villains lounging by the swimming pools of Bel Air as in the waterfront dives of San Pedro. In his essay in *The Simple Art of Murder* Chandler described Marlowe's mission in those familiar words that have now become the standard ethos of film-noir heroes: "Down these mean streets a man must go who is not himself mean, who is neither tarnished nor afraid." He went on to discuss the importance of honor, and concluded the passage: "If there were enough like him, the world would be a very safe place to live in, without becoming too dull to be worth living in."

Uniquely, Humphrey Bogart played both of the most celebrated detectives in American crime fiction, in films that would become classics of film noir. Huston and Hawks approached their material differently. *The Maltese Falcon* is for all its red herrings and false trails tightly plotted and ultimately logical. By contrast there is nothing claustrophobic about *The Big Sleep*, and the discursive narrative roams, taking Marlowe far beyond his walk-up office as he picks his way through a corrupt labyrinth of gamblers, blackmailers, pornographers, hired thugs, and murderers. The storyline is so loose that not all the bodies are ever properly explained. Hawks himself became so confused that he asked Chandler who exactly was responsible for one of the corpses, but the author was unable to offer any explanation so the director left it as an unresolved plot-hole which, given the film's pace and intricacy, went unnoticed. The released version of the film differed from the initial print, and contained re-shot and fresh material produced several months after initial production had ended. The reason was that during the earlier filming *To Have and Have Not* had opened to outstanding business, and Warner soon realized that Bogart and Bacall had become a formidable box-office combination. In recent years it has been possible to view Hawks's first thoughts, and compare the two versions. The second is lighter and undoubtedly more fun, but strays even further from plot logic.

The reason for capitalizing on Bacall's presence made sound commercial sense. Sexuality was an essential element of the film. Marlowe is presented as hugely appealing to women, and Bogart, by now in his mid-forties, exuded an easy confidence that was entirely plausible, assisted by the fact that he and Bacall, then twenty, had married in May 1945. Their rapport comes across vividly on screen. Marlowe, is hired to investigate an employee's disappearance by General Sternwood, a formidable but immobilized old warrior who eccentrically conducts the interview in his hothouse. He encounters the two daughters, Vivian (Bacall) with whom a teasing flirtation is soon overtaken by mutual passion, and the wayward, drugged-up, thumb-sucking Carmen (Martha Vickers) who assails him with a nymphomaniac's zeal. Everywhere Marlowe goes women seem taken with him, be they hatcheck girls, female taxi drivers, or most delightfully, the young proprietress of a bookstore (Dorothy Malone) who closes up shop for him. Only a hoity-toity woman in charge of an art gallery, a front for shady dealings, fails to succumb, when he enters absurdly disguising himself as a connoisseur but almost immediately blowing his cover by mispronouncing the word "ceramics."

If *The Big Sleep* endures it is on account of its wit, verve, and evocation of the nocturnal city, but particularly for Bogart's compelling, perfectly judged central performance.

"Vivian: I don't like your manners. Marlowe: And I'm not crazy about yours. I didn't ask to see you. I don't mind if you don't like my manners. I don't like them myself. They are pretty bad. I grieve over them on long winter evenings. I don't mind your ritzing me drinking your lunch out of a bottle. But don't waste your time trying to cross-examine me."

Bogart and Bacall cross-talk in *The Big Sleep*

Bogart, Bacall in *The Big Sleep*.　　　　Studio portrait, *The Big Sleep*.

Philip Marlowe (Bogart) and Vivian Sternwood (Bacall).

Dorothy Malone as bookshop manager with Bogart.

Near showdown in *The Big Sleep*.

Dead Reckoning (1947)

Another film noir, made on the run at another studio on a loan-out in order to cash in on Bogart's popularity. It was originally intended to have Rita Hayworth play the shady female lead. Lizabeth Scott is no Mary Astor, but she has a deep husky voice, like Bacall. Bogart is the hard-boiled friend of her victim, and exchanges dialogue that sounds as though it has been recycled from better films. "You're going to fry," sounds less appealing than his remark "Yes angel, I'm going to send you over" in *The Maltese Falcon*. Bogart's story is narrated in flashback to a priest.

The Two Mrs Carrolls (1947)

Delayed for two years, perhaps in the hope that Bogart's stature would have grown sufficiently to enable his miscalculated casting to be swallowed by an enthusiastic public, it still qualifies as one of his worst films. He plays an artist living in England who paints his wife as "the Angel of Death" and poisons her. He marries again, this time to Barbara Stanwyck, and seems set to repeat his squalid trick, but discovers to his cost that she is smarter than he thinks. The provenance is a 1935 stage play, and must have seemed tired even then.

Dark Passage (1947)

In his third teaming with Bacall, Bogart plays a framed wife-murderer who escapes from San Quentin, determined to make those responsible for his incarceration pay. He is harbored by Bacall, who believes in his innocence, having seen a similar failure of justice in her late father's case, and keeps him in her San Francisco apartment, his head swathed in bandages after some deft plastic surgery. For the first hour Bogart has little to act with, not even nostrils, and his earlier scenes are shot with subjective camerawork, as though through his eyes. Agnes Moorhead, venomous as a well-dressed harpy, comes close to stealing the acting accolades in this implausible, thin melodrama.

"Bogie and I made our third movie together – Dark Passage – and went to San Francisco for a month of location shooting... I became aware of Bogie's nerves – if the phone rang, he'd tense up, didn't want to answer it, didn't want to speak to any except the closest. He'd noticed a bare spot on his cheek where his beard was not growing. The one spot increased to several – then he'd wake in the morning and find clumps of hair on the pillow. That alarmed him... The more hair fell out, the more nervous he got, and the more nervous he got, the more hair fell out. In the last scene of Dark Passage he wore a complete wig."

Lauren Bacall, *By Myself and Then Some*

Always Together (1947)

Another unbilled cameo performance by Bogart in a film in which the heroine imagines herself in dream sequences with her favorite movie stars.

Bacall and Bogart in *Dark Passage*.

The Treasure of the Sierra Madre (1947)

For his second film with Bogart, the director John Huston returned to the theme of greed, but in a context far removed from that of *The Maltese Falcon*. Set in Mexico, where it was largely filmed on location, it follows the attempt of a trio of indigent Americans for a gold strike on a remote mountain. Bogart, as Dobbs, is a down-and-out who amusingly in early scenes in Tampico panhandles the same smartly attired fellow-American three times in as many hours (a cameo by Huston himself). Tim Holt is Curtin, a younger man, still relatively untried by life, but like Dobbs destitute after working for a swindling contractor. Assisted by Dobbs unexpectedly winning lottery money, they join forces with Howard, an old-timer who knows about gold prospecting. Howard is played by Huston's father Walter, and both father and son were to win Oscars for their work on the film.

The old man never seems to stop talking and is constantly mouthing through his toothless gums an unceasing stream of homespun philosophy, which may sound half-baked but is oddly prescient, as events eventually show. He knows a thing or two about the corrosive effect gold has on a man's psyche. "Ah, as long as there's no find, the noble brotherhood will last but when the piles of gold begin to grow ... that's when the trouble starts."

The journey to the mountain is perilous. Tensions arise within, and the party is attacked by bandits. They find their target, work the gold and amass enough to give each a fortune. That is when trouble really strikes. Suspicion becomes paranoia. Greed becomes the prime motivator. Bogart has to portray a man driven into unreason and hatred—and willing to commit murder to enhance his share. His moral disintegration is finely realized and is one of the highlights of his career. The film has a doubly ironic ending in that only Dobbs dies, and the gold dust is stolen by the bandits who are unaware of its value, and allow it to blow away into the wilderness.

Downbeat endings are alleged to be unpopular, and that belief was sustained here when the film attracted disappointing audiences in spite of some excellent reviews. The lack of romantic interest was another factor cited for its poor performance, although it would have been inappropriate to the story. Tantalizingly, Ann Sheridan, one of Warner's most glamorous stars, is briefly glimpsed early in the film making an unbilled appearance as a prostitute.

It was by no means a flawless work. Because of a budgetary overrun the production was called back from Mexico to shoot in the controlled conditions of Burbank, and some of the outdoor scenes bear the unmistakable look of studio back projection. Max Steiner furnished perhaps his most plangent score since *Gone With the Wind*, an insistent theme that seems to dog every footstep of the trek. The expository opening scenes go on too long, and the journey does not begin until well into the film. Walter Huston attracted acclaim for his flamboyant performance, even though it is in some measure irritating and hammy. Bogart does what is required of him, and does it well, with his characteristic professionalism.

"My father and his friends were capable of mischief. Once, after John Huston and his father, Walter, got Academy Awards for their work in **The Treasure of the Sierra Madre**, Dad, who also got an Oscar nomination for the movie, went back to John Huston's place where Bogie and the director, still wearing tuxedos, played football in the mud against a movie executive and a screenwriter. They either didn't have a football or were too drunk to look for one, so, instead they ran pass patterns with a grapefruit."

Stephen Bogart, *Bogart: In Search of My Father*

Bogart as Fred C. Dobbs,
The Treasure of the Sierra Madre.

Following Pages: Tim Holt, Bogart, Walter Huston on the quest for *The Treasure of the Sierra Madre.*

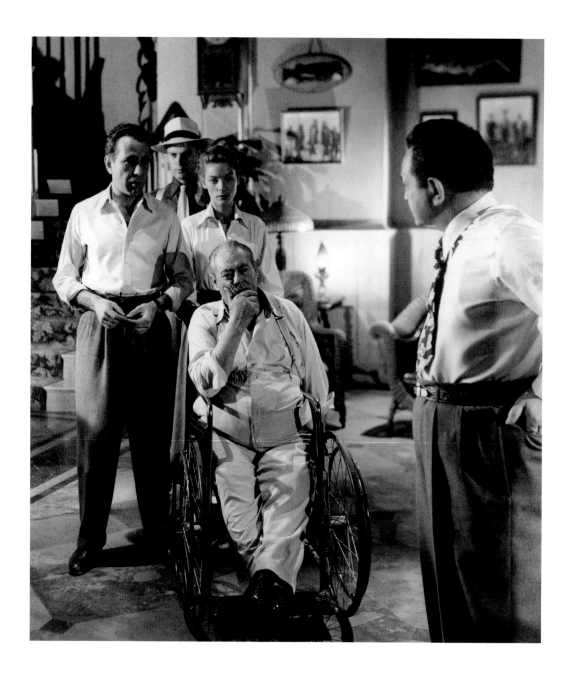

Key Largo (1948)

Bogart is a disillusioned army major who visits a hotel in the Florida Keys, the chain of causeway-linked islands that curve ninety miles south of the mainland into the Gulf of Mexico. He intends to console the widow (Bacall) and father (Lionel Barrymore) of a comrade lost in wartime. A fugitive gangster (Edward G. Robinson) arrives and his entourage holds everyone hostage as a hurricane strikes. Bogart is expected to deal with the murderous mobster but initially is reluctant, not so much for conscientious reasons but because the odds are against him. It is like *The Petrified Forest* revisited, recast and in a new setting, but is similarly derived from a wordy Broadway drama. Huston incorporates an exciting action climax at sea as Robinson forces Bogart to take him by boat to Cuba. Claire Trevor as the gangster's alcoholic moll has a memorable scene of humiliation when she is forced to sing "Moanin' Low" to an unwilling audience. It was the last time Bacall and Bogart would appear in a film together, and is a satisfying envoi.

Bogart, Harry Lewis, Bacall, Lionel Barrymore,
Edward G. Robinson, *Key Largo.*

Bacall, Bogart as hostages to Robinson.

Previous Pages: Bogart and Bacall, John Huston between them in the background.

Bogart and Bacall on *Key Largo* set.

Bogart, Dan Seymour, Harry Lewis in *Key Largo*.   Bogart, Lewis, Seymour and Robinson.

Knock On Any Door (1949)

John Derek makes his debut as a delinquent who has murdered a policeman, a role that Brando had declined. Bogart is his hotshot defending attorney, whose own background in the same slums gives him a unique voice in expressing his client's feelings, and the low tactics employed by the harsh prosecutor (George Macready) help him win the jury's sympathy. Unfortunately for his case the boy, in spite of his clean-cut appearance and polite manner, is guilty, and is tricked into admitting it. The social message—that crime derives from brutalizing conditions—now seems dated and trite but Nicholas Ray, who was to make a specialty of at-odds loners (*Rebel Without a Cause*) directs with spirit. Bogart took no credit as executive producer.

Andrew Morton: Until we do away with the type of neighborhood that produced this boy, ten will spring up to take his place, a hundred, a thousand. Until we wipe out the slums and rebuild them, knock on any door and you may find Nick Romano.

Bogart as idealist attorney in *Knock On Any Door*

Tokyo Joe (1949)

In the first American film set in postwar Japan, Bogart is a former nightclub owner who has become an ace fighter pilot for the Allies. He returns to Tokyo to find his White Russian wife is still alive, but remarried. She was coerced into making Japanese propaganda broadcasts. To prevent her arrest he agrees to ferry war criminals back into Japan for a sinister baron who kidnaps his child to make sure he does. He dies heroically, rescuing her, and thwarting the evil plan. Again a Bogart-inspired production, but it is sadly disappointing and melodramatic.

"Bogart backed the shallow adventure movie (**Tokyo Joe**) but his heart wasn't in it. His heroic rescue is flat and predictable, and he seems to have walked through the part like a public figure playing a theatrical version of himself."

Jeffrey Meyers, *Bogart: A Life in Hollywood*

Bogart in *Tokyo Joe*.

1950—1956

Children only arrived with Bogart's fourth marriage. Stephen Humphrey was born on January 6, 1949, taking the name Steve from the character his father played in *To Have and Have Not*. His sister Leslie Howard entered the family on August 23, 1952. She was named in tribute to the actor who had given Bogart his first big break by insisting he play Duke Mantee on film. Fatherhood was not an easy role for him, not helped by his huge celebrity and constant working. In domestic matters Lauren Bacall was the driving force, and although Jewish sent the children to the Episcopalian Sunday school. Their home was now a sizeable house on South Mapleton Drive in the Holmby Hills.

Having severed his Warner relationship, Bogart was unable to cast Bacall in a Santana film as she was still tied into her contract with the old studio. Initially he was wary of playing opposite Katharine Hepburn in John Huston's *The African Queen*, sensing that she would be out of her element. Huston loved arduous locations and it was the longest, hardest shoot of his life, much of it in the then Congo in remote, sweltering, bug-infested swamps that made him ruefully recall the comparative ease of *The Treasure of the Sierra Madre*. His fears concerning Hepburn were groundless. Playing social opposites obliged by a common purpose to share their fates, their on-screen rapport proved immensely popular with audiences, and for the first and only time—in spite of four nominations—Bogart won the Academy Award for Best Actor.

The last of his six films directed by John Huston was *Beat the Devil*, purportedly a joke at the expense of Hollywood, but one that backfired in that audiences seemed unready to appreciate it. As Bogart unwisely had much of his own money in it, it is clear why the association came to an end. In some respects it is like *The Maltese Falcon* re-enacted in the sumptuously sunlit Mediterranean fishing-port of Ravello, with a cast seemingly unaware of the next page of the screenplay, but nevertheless determined to enjoy the scenery. An undoubted folly, it has an idiosyncratic appeal.

Bogart restored the gravitas with his next role, that of Queeg, the paranoid minesweeper captain forcibly relieved of his command during a storm at sea in World War II, in the adaptation of Herman Wouk's *The Caine Mutiny*. To secure naval co-operation a title had to be inserted suggesting that no officer could ever have behaved as he did. Mutinies do not occur in the U.S. Navy. The classic scene is his performance at the court martial of Van Johnson, blamed for leading the mutiny, in which the "by-the-book" sea-salt reveals himself too damaged to lead men, but even more effective is a wardroom scene in which he asks his officers for their loyalty and is spurned.

Bogart in 1952, with apocalyptic backdrop.

Billy Wilder's *Sabrina* was a less rewarding experience. An unlikely late substitute for Cary Grant, he did not get on well with either Wilder or his co-star William Holden, and was skeptical with regard to Audrey Hepburn, whose acting technique failed to impress him. The final batch of films fell far short of his talents, although some gave him moments in which his flair still showed. These include *The Barefoot Contessa*, in which his romanticism spurs him in the projection of Ava Gardner as a popular idol, and *The Desperate Hours* where he plays an ageing convict and hostage-taker disguising his vulnerability with ferocious cruelty.

After *The Harder They Fall* he could make no more films. Diagnosed with cancer of the oesophagus, he was subjected to drastic surgery and treatments which, compared with modern medical standards, were crude and ineffective. Warned by his doctors that he should curb his tastes for alcohol and cigarettes he ignored the former and switched to filters for the latter. At that time in the 1950s an association between smoking and cancer had yet to be made public. During the last, increasingly depressing months of his life he stayed home at South Mapleton Drive, receiving visitors as though enduring a temporary setback, but when he made his last outing on his beloved *Santana* the realization that he was not going to survive must have been clear to him. A dumbwaiter was adapted in his house to enable him to ascend to the second story without having to use the stairs; it necessitated a claustrophobic passage in a cramped space that must have distressed him. He raged when a newspaper columnist announced that he was in a hospital fighting for his life, and composed a belligerent missive "an open letter to the working press." In it he wrote: "I'm a better man than I ever was—and all I need now is about thirty pounds in weight which I am sure some of you can spare." His friends, among them Huston, Spencer Tracy and Katharine Hepburn, David Niven and his wife, Frank Sinatra, Raymond Massey, and many others called often.

His condition worsened that Christmas, and he was unable to drink his birthday health. On January 13, 1957 he drifted into a coma. In the night at 2.25 a.m. his nurse woke Bacall to tell her that he had died gently in his sleep. His last words to his wife the previous afternoon had been "Goodbye kid. Hurry back."

Humphrey Bogart was only fifty-seven when he died. His son had just turned eight, his daughter was four. His demise was greatly mourned throughout the world. In the passage of years he seems to have become an enduring presence, an immediately recognizable icon to generations born since. Of all the stars of Hollywood's so-called Golden Age he represents a tangible, relevant strength. He perfectly embodied some of the simple, admirable qualities once held to distinguish the American character, such as a capable self-sufficiency and a refusal to be pushed around. In a handful of the many films he made he projected a romantic edge, sometimes in the most surprising contexts. As an actor he was authoritative, professional, and secure. In his life as well as in his screen persona, Bogie was his own man.

Bogart as Dixon Steele, *In a Lonely Place*.

Chain Lightning (1950)

The time-worn test pilot plot was resuscitated and updated to embrace the new jet age, but to little effect. Bogart plays an ex-wartime bomber pilot hired by an unprincipled manufacturer (Raymond Massey) to try out a new aircraft. There is a love triangle with its designer, Richard Whorf, and Eleanor Parker, Massey's secretary. Whorf is killed testing a new ejection seat, and Bogart defies orders by carrying out the same experiment. The flat direction and trite screenplay are factors that render the film uninvolving, and even Bogart has a struggle to keep interest alive.

In a Lonely Place (1950)

In a milieu close to home Bogart plays a screenwriter, Dixon Steele, bitterly aware that his early success counts for little after a row of box-office failures. Asked to adapt a current bestseller, which he regards with contempt, he refuses to read it and instead has a coatcheck girl explain the plot to him after hours in his apartment. When she has finished he sends her into the night with $20 to find a cab. The next day an old army friend, now a detective, calls and asks him to go with him to see his captain at the Beverly Hills police department. The girl's strangled body has been found dumped off a lonely highway, and both policemen are struck by his lack of surprise or emotion at the revelation. Laurel, a new neighbor (Gloria Grahame) in an apartment across the courtyard from his, attests that she saw the girl leave alone, supporting his story. The captain, having looked at Steele's record for violent, drunken outbursts that have caused physical damage to others, is quite sure he has found his man. Meanwhile Steele and Laurel fall into each other's arms. She is a failed actress bruised by experience, and each of them finds a new, gentle strength in the relationship.

He resumes writing and with her encouragement produces a brilliant screenplay. The police are still probing however, and their tactics cause his short-fused anger to erupt into terrifying and uncontrolled ferocity, leading her to wonder if he really is a murderer. She tries to flee, he moves to stop her and seems on the point of strangling her. The telephone interrupts. It is the police to say that the real murderer has confessed and they offer their apologies. It is too late. As a couple they are finished. As he walks out of her life she wistfully recalls a line of his he had wanted to incorporate in his screenplay: "I lived a few weeks when you loved me."

The character portrayed by Bogart is not particularly attractive. He is cynical and filled with self-loathing, He seems ever ready to take umbrage and pick quarrels, often deliberately antagonizing people. He treats his few remaining friends with scorn and indifference. He is particularly cruel to Mel (Art Smith), his loyal agent, and in a rage punches him in the face, smashing his glasses. He has destroyed a former relationship by breaking the woman's nose. The police, not quite comprehending how he can invite a girl back to his apartment late at night without sexual intentions, ask quite reasonably why he could not have called for a cab instead of sending her out to look for one, and he has no answer. His morbid interest in the killer's technique, which so horrifies the well-raised young wife of his detective friend, could be explained as a writer's professional interest, but there is no excuse for the vicious beating he hands out to a young man who has had the temerity to complain after his car has been hit by an angry Steele who has just run through a STOP sign. Only the intervention of a shocked Laurel prevents from smashing a rock into his skull.

The pessimism of Ray's film and the ambiguity of the central character left audiences unimpressed and *In a Lonely Place* was a box-office failure, in spite of a number of critics appreciating the quality of performance and intelligence of the script and direction. Bogart, it seemed, was acceptable to the public as a romantic hero who is outwardly tough, inwardly noble. He was also well regarded when he played irredeemable villains. A shaded, flawed character such as Dixon Steele was seen to be too subtle to be approved, and the film languished until a later generation, aware of the maverick positioning of Ray in the generally bland context of 1950s American cinema, elevated it to one of the most important in the Bogart corpus of work. He was not particularly fond of it, in spite of it being produced by his company. He had wanted Bacall for the female lead, but Warner refused to release her form her contract. Gloria Grahame excelled in the role, and it was probably her best acting performance. She was in the late throes of her declining marriage to Nicholas Ray at the time.

The Enforcer (1951)

In the United Kingdom it retained its original, more apt title, *Murder, Inc.* Raoul Walsh, uncredited, was responsible for much of the direction of the last film Bogart was to make for Warner, taking over when its original director became seriously ill. It is something of a throwback to an earlier era. Bogart plays an assistant district attorney whose task it is to bring to account the organizers of a notorious syndicate, and his manifold duties outside the courtroom appear to be witness protection, police investigation, and gunning down lurking hitmen. Ted de Corsia is a notable worried heavy. Shot with pace and economy, it even offers echoes of Warner's social conscience, a staple of studio output in the 1930s.

Sirocco (1951)

In French-controlled Damascus in the mid-1920s, Bogart is an ex-saloonkeeper turned gun-unner who is supplying arms to Syrian rebels. His adversary is a colonel of intelligence (Lee J. Cobb) whose mistress (Marta Toren) interests him. Financially it was the least successful of the four Santana productions, and was handicapped by its passing similarity to *Casablanca*, marred by the distinctly ignoble character of Bogart in this instance, and his sticky end from a grenade, quite probably deriving from his own merchandise.

Bogart in *Sirocco*.

The African Queen (1951)

The inspired pairing of Katharine Hepburn and Humphrey Bogart resulted in one of the most popular films of all time. They were not first choices. Years earlier C. S. Forester's story had been proposed for Bette Davis, first with David Niven, later with James Mason. It is unlikely that same serendipity would have prevailed. The producer Sam Spiegel and John Huston acquired the rights and convinced Bogart that he would be right for the lead with Hepburn. With his old friend Huston directing Bogart was in a happy frame of mind, and although he and Hepburn had never worked together before, the combination was admirable. The attraction of opposites was central to the film, an unusual love story set in German East Africa after the commencement of World War I. She played Rose, a doughty, strong-willed, middle-aged spinster who with her older brother (Robert Morley) runs a mission in an upriver village. He is Charlie Allnut, a scruffy, gin-drinking water rat who brings their supplies in his wheezing, decrepit riverboat *African Queen*. The Germans sack and destroy the village and her broken brother dies. Charlie offers to ferry her to safety, but she devises a hare-brained scheme to sail down the seemingly un-navigable river to a large lake controlled by a German gunboat, and use the *Queen* and its cargo of explosives as a guided missile to destroy it. The journey is a series of perilous adventures with storms, insects, swamps, rapids, enemy sharpshooters, and mechanical breakdowns, but shared adversity turns the unlikely pair into lovers. After the final failure of their plan and their capture, and just before they are about to be hanged on the deck of their target, she persuades the German captain to marry them so that they can enter eternity as man and wife. There is one last, and entirely fitting, surprise.

Forester's story, written shortly before the emergence of his famous naval hero of the Napoleonic Wars, Captain Horatio Hornblower, was a straightforward, unromantic, and definitely unhumorous yarn. Huston's film is warm, often humorous, occasionally uproariously funny, for instance in the early scene where Bogart, called upon to take genteel tea with the missionary and his sister, is unable to stop his stomach rumbling like an out-of-control beer truck. Charlie as conceived by Forester was a cockney, but in Bogart's hands he becomes a Canadian, although if he makes concessions to an accent they are imperceptible. Much of the film was shot on location in what was then the Belgian Congo, often in extremely hazardous and primitive living conditions. Almost everyone went down with dysentery from tainted water, and Hepburn was a particular victim, even though she adapted to life in the wild with an ease that fascinated Bogart. "She doesn't drink, and she breezes through it all as if it were a weekend in Connecticut." Huston and Bogart however somehow seemed miraculously unscathed from stomach bugs, and it was attributed to their refusal to savor the water, preferring to rely on neat Scotch.

The rest of the film was made in the United Kingdom, the first time that Bogart had worked in British studios. It was also his first film in color, and the cinematography was under the aegis of the brilliant Jack Cardiff, who had shot *The Red Shoes* for Michael Powell and Emeric Pressburger. For Bogart probably the most significant consequence of *The African Queen* was the winning of the Academy Award for Best Actor, his only Oscar.

"John had spoken to Bogie about *The African Queen*... Bogie liked his life as it was; going to New York was all the traveling he wanted to do. Finally Sam Spiegel told Katharine Hepburn that he had Bogie and John – told John that he had Bogie and Katie – told Bogie that had John and Katie – and *The African Queen* was put together. I was wildly excited but Bogie knew that John would find the most inaccessible spot in Africa as a location and he dreaded it."

Lauren Bacall, *By Myself and Then Some*

Bogart as Charlie Allnut in *The African Queen*. | Katharine Hepburn teamed with Bogart, *The African Queen*.

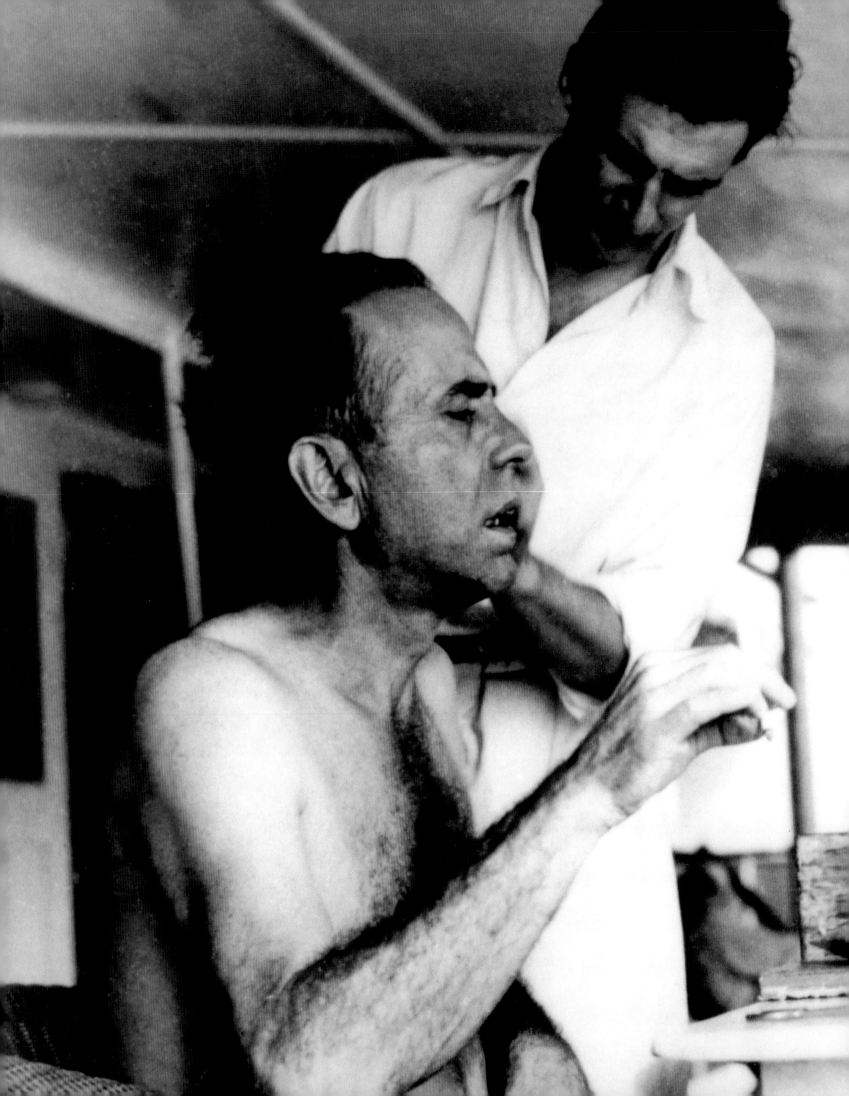

Deadline – U.S.A. (1952)

Bogart once again plays the crusader, here a newspaper editor whose owner (Ethel Barrymore), the founder's widow, is going to sell out to a rival. He is beset with justifying its continued existence, and using the exposure of a crime baron (Martin Gabel) as his big cause. He is also trying to deal with his ex-wife (Kim Hunter) and her new fiancé. In spite of documentary-style footage shot at the New York *Daily News* the newspaper atmosphere is not entirely convincing, much in the same way that the title is meaningless to journalists (Dateline surely?)

Road to Bali (1952)

A clip of Bogart pulling *The African Queen* through the swamp is included as a sight gag in this Bing Crosby-Bob Hope-Dorothy Lamour comedy.

Battle Circus (1953)

During the Korean War the setting is a Mobile Army Surgical Hospital. The film's original title was going be M.A.S.H., which might have changed film and television history, since this romantic drama is light years from Robert Altman's irreverent, sex-obsessed 1970 satire. Bogart is a dedicated surgeon whose marital problems cause him to drink too much, and June Allyson is an army nurse with whom he finds comfort and eventually love. It is for Richard Brooks, who directed, a slight film, and is marred by Allyson's casting. Usually excellent in lightweight, frothy comedies and musicals, here she flounders out of her depth.

Beat the Devil (1953)

If there is an air of spontaneity to this sunlit comedy it would be understandable, since the screenplay was being written by the director and the impish, literary *enfant terrible* Truman Capote on a day-to-basis, with the cast invariably not knowing what was to happen next. An ill-matched assortment of shady characters, including Robert Morley and Peter Lorre, are holed-up in the picturesque Campanian coastal village of Ravello, waiting for a ship to take them to Africa. A caper is afoot, something involving land and uranium deposits. Jennifer Jones in a blonde wig is hilarious as a fake Englishwoman married to the pukka Edward Underdown, but very much taken with an American, Bogart— whose glamorous Anglophile wife Gina Lollobrigida similarly has eyes on her husband. A box-office loser, it now enjoys cult status.

The Love Lottery (1954)

Humphrey Bogart in an Ealing comedy? At the conclusion of this David Niven—Peggy Cummins film he makes an unexpected cameo appearance as a joke. Sadly *The Love Lottery* is not Ealing at its best, so it is nobody's finest hour.

Previous Pages: On location for *The African Queen* with moral support from Lauren Bacall.

Bogart in *Deadline U.S.A.*

With June Allyson in *Battle Circus.*

The Caine Mutiny (1954)

The paranoid Captain Queeg was a naval martinet created by the novelist Herman Wouk for his 1951 bestseller. A series of pettifogging obsessions with trivial matters leads to low crew morale and danger to the ship, and officers relieve him of his command. At the court martial Queeg, initially confident, is destroyed under cross-examination, reduced to a burbling wreck as he compulsively clicks a pair of large ball bearings in his hand. The stage version focused entirely on the courtroom, leaving doubt over Queeg's insanity, but the film offers no leeway. Bogart is, however, brilliant in his portrayal.

Captain Queeg: Aboard my ship, excellent performance is standard, standard performance is sub-standard, and sub-standard performance is not permitted to exist – that, I warn you.

Bogart in The Caine Mutiny

As Captain Queeg in *The Caine Mutiny*.

With Van Johnson on the U.S.S. *Caine* bridge.

Sabrina (1954)

Billy Wilder, having lost Cary Grant, asked Bogart to step into this sophisticated comedy in the role of the elder of two wealthy brothers on a Long Island estate. His sibling, William Holden, is something of a feckless playboy, while he has a corporate brain and keeps the family finances bubbling. The strategy of marrying Holden off to a well-connected socialite (Martha Hyer) is threatened when he falls instead for their chauffeur's daughter (Audrey Hepburn), who has been transformed into a desirable beauty by a sojourn in Paris. Bogart sets himself up as a decoy to entice her away, but finds that he is similarly smitten. He is assured but lacks the lightness of touch that Grant would have provided.

The Barefoot Contessa (1954)

From the slums of Madrid comes Ava Gardner, turned into a movie star by a loud press agent (Edmond O'Brien) and a drunken, faded director (Bogart) who see her in a cabaret. Her career is meteoric and brings about his return to favor. She marries an Italian aristocrat (Rosanno Brazzi), and finds he is impotent. Later Brazzi shoots her and a lover, and dramatic her story is told by Bogart in flashback from her graveside. Mankiewicz may have been hoping that his overwrought yet dull film would do for the movies what his Oscar-winning *All About Eve* had done for theater, but he was sadly disappointed.

Billy Wilder directs Audrey Hepburn and Bogart, *Sabrina*. | On location with Ava Gardner, *The Barefoot Contessa* .

We're No Angels (1955)

Three convicts escape from Devil's Island and besiege a shopkeeper and his wife (Leo G. Carroll, Joan Bennett) on Christmas Eve. It may have echoes of Bogart's earlier film directed by Michael Curtiz, *Passage to Marseille*, but it soon turns into an amiable comedy in which the trio (Bogart, Aldo Ray, and Peter Ustinov) are so disgusted by the wiles of Basil Rathbone as the nasty landlord, that they stay to help sort out the family troubles. Originally a successful stage play, it is over-egged by Curtiz's direction, and fails to satisfy.

The Left Hand of God (1955)

Bogart plays an American flyer who has crashed in a remote part of China during the war, and has played along with the local warlord (Lee J. Cobb). Desiring eventually to return home, he adopts the disguise of a Catholic priest, but during his escape finds that he is obliged to minister to a stricken village as though he were a genuine man of the cloth. Gene Tierney, a mission nurse, is attracted to him in spite of his collar, and he resolves to reveal his subterfuge. It was Bogart's only film in CinemaScope, but otherwise unremarkable.

Peter Ustinov and Bogart, *We're No Angels*.

Bogart as bogus priest in *The Left Hand of God*.

The Desperate Hours (1955)

A ruthless killer breaks jail with his younger brother and another convict, and takes over a comfortable suburban home in a quiet neighborhood, holding its occupants hostage. Glenn Griffin—cruel, crude, and driven by a need for revenge—is the last of Bogart's studies of a psychopath. On Broadway the role was played by Paul Newman, with Karl Malden as the beleaguered householder, but to allow Bogart to take over, the part was adapted to match his age. He had wanted his old friend Spencer Tracy as the householder but had to settle for Frederic March who is solid, but less interesting. Wyler's direction is controlled and careful, sustaining the tension, although the plot device of having March go to his business as if everything is normal strikes a note of implausibility.

"They didn't let people know it was a gangster film. Maybe it's because of Mom-ism these days and no one cares if Pop is in danger of having his head bashed in."

Bogart on *The Desperate Hours*

Marisa Pavan and Bogart, *The Desperate Hours* (1955).

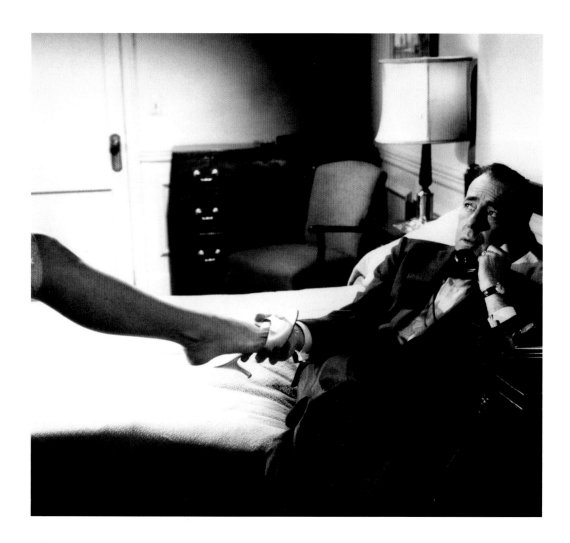

The Harder They Fall (1956)

In his final film Bogart plays a fired sports columnist who is sucked into working for a shady boxing promoter (Rod Steiger). His task is to push a mountainous but untalented Argentinian boxer to championship status via a string of rigged contests. Eventually his conscience asserts itself, and in spite of all the risks he exposes the racket in print. Bogart's illness is reflected in his aged appearance, and his always husky voice sometimes sounds like a deep croak. Steiger is dazzling, giving an authoritative, controlled performance that seems to be challenging Bogart's crown, but the battle is in reality a tie.

Eddie Willis: What do you care what a bunch of bloodthirsty, screaming people think of you? Did you ever get a look at their faces? They pay a few lousy bucks hoping to see a man get killed. To hell with them! Think of yourself. Get your money and get out of this rotten business.

Bogart in *The Harder They Fall*, his last film

Last film: *The Harder they Fall.*

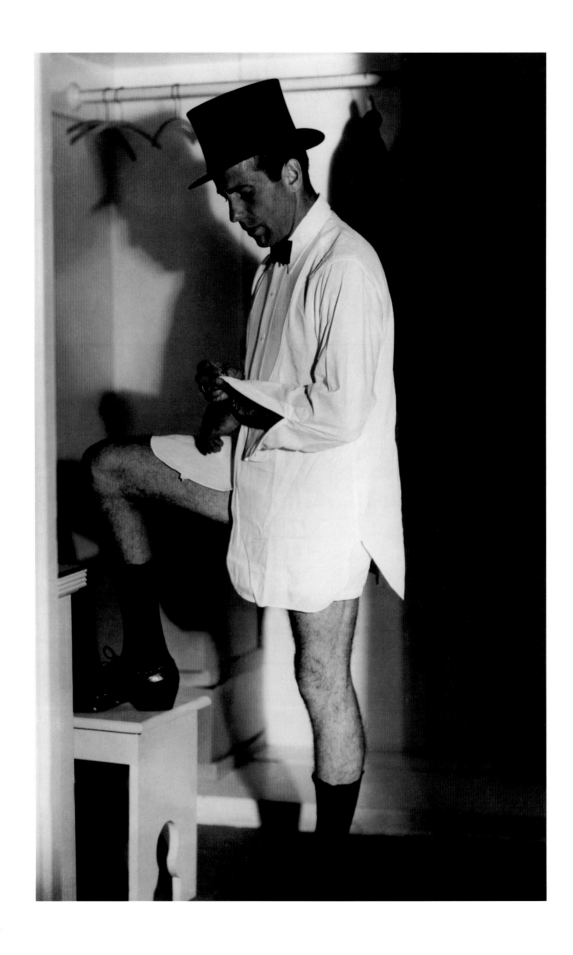

Epitaph for a Tough Guy by Alistair Cooke

Alistair Cooke, who until he died in 2004 served as a cultural ambassador for America for over sixty years, was chief American correspondent for the *Guardian* when he first met Bogart and Bacall while covering the Eisenhower/Stevenson presidential campaign in 1952. The Bogarts were Democrats and friends and supporters of Adlai Stevenson, and had turned out on the campaign train on its last lap through New England. Over drinks on board the Cooke/Bogart friendship was established. "From the afternoon of that first drink till the day of his death, I found him an original quite unlike any other human being I have known," Cooke wrote in what was to become a defining profile contained in his book *Six Men*. This extract recalls the last days of the actor.

———

One is always reading, in obituaries, of some bold good man who could not abide cant and fearlessly denounced it. Bogart never bothered to denounce it since, no matter how meek its disguise, it was as plainly offensive to him as a bad smell. And his hypersensitiveness to the faintest aura of pomp made him an impossible man to make up to, to cozen or impress. Many first acquaintances were dropped at once when, out of shyness probably, they tried to adopt some of the Bogart bluster in the hope of showing right away that they were his sort. One of his own sort was enough for him. He took to many unlikely types and immediately tended to admire people who, however quaint, were nobody but themselves. He did not require a woman to appear knowing, an Englishman to rough up his accent, or anyone to buddy up to him by telling a so-called dirty story. This last gesture was a fatal mistake: Bogart detested dirty stories and shut up like a clam. You could say also that he was socially difficult in that he was impatient of compliments and perfunctory praise. He had the deadly insight that one meets with in some drunks (and that one hopes not to meet with in most schizophrenics) who are beginning to get troublesome and whom you hope to appease with cordial approaches. Such psychics pause long enough in their garrulousness to say firmly, "You don't like me, do you?" So Bogart was not a man ever to flatter or—what was harder in his last year—to sympathise with.

Before I saw him for the last time, in the late spring of 1956, I had had from a surgeon friend the dimmest prognosis of his condition, which was that of a man still receiving massive doses of X-ray treatment after an operation for cancer of the oesophagus. "Cancer of the oesophagus," my friend told me, "has a mortality rate of 100 per cent." I was sorry to have

The "socially difficult" Bogart dresses up for the evening.

heard this, for it was going to be hard to keep up the usual banter. But it turned out that there was no strain of any kind because, I believe, he knew the worst and had months before resolved to rouse himself for two hours a day to relax with a few intimate friends before the end came. Most of us never knew for sure that he had been for many months in abominable pain. Another of his triumphant deceptions was that he managed to convince everybody that he was only intermittently uncomfortable. Throughout the spring, he remained a genial skeleton and when I went up there the last time, at the beginning of June, his wife was off talking to a journalist friend, and a lawyer was leaving Bogart, who had just finished making his will. Whether his wife knew about this I am unsure, but he spoke of it to me, and of his illness, and the sudden uselessness of money, with an entirely unforced humour and an equally unforced seriousness; neither with complaint nor with a brave absence of complaint.

Two of his oldest friends came in, Nunnally Johnson and David Niven, and we talked about the coming California primary election, which pitted Senator Estes Kefauver against Adlai Stevenson in the knock-out bout for the 1956 Democratic presidential nomination. The popular reputation of Senator—especially among Stevenson supporters—was that of an earnest, wily, straitlaced and rather sanctimonious South preacher. It seemed a good time to enlighten the assembled company to Kefauver's quite different reputation in the exclusive club of the United States Senate. "True or not," I said, "he has a terrific reputation as a lecher." Bogart nodded as if to say it was no more than you'd expect. Nunnally Johnson was a little more alert and suspected he'd misheard: "Did you say lecturer?" "No, I said 'lecher!'" "My God," Bogart cried, "lecher! I wish to God we could spread the same word about Adlai."

It was, if not a happy occasion, at least a serene and cheerful one. And I was aware of no strain on the part of the company. It is difficult for actors to avoid the dramatising of their emotional life, whether grossly by "living the part" or subtly by sentimental deprecation. Bogart, it was a vast relief to discover, was merely himself, a brave man who had come to terms, as we all may pray to do, with the certain approach of death.

In short, a much more intelligent man than most of his trade; or several others, a touchy man who found the world more corrupt than he had hoped; a man with a tough shell hiding a fine, core. He had transmuted his own character into a film persona and imposed it on a world impatient of men more obviously good. By showily neglecting the outward forms of grace, he kept inferior men at a distance. For he lived in a town crowded with malign flatterers, hypocrites and poseurs, fake ascetics, studio panders and the pimps of the press. From all of them he was determined to keep his secret: the rather shameful secret in the realistic world we inhabit, of being an incurable puritan, gentle at bottom and afraid to seem so.

Bogart in 1942.

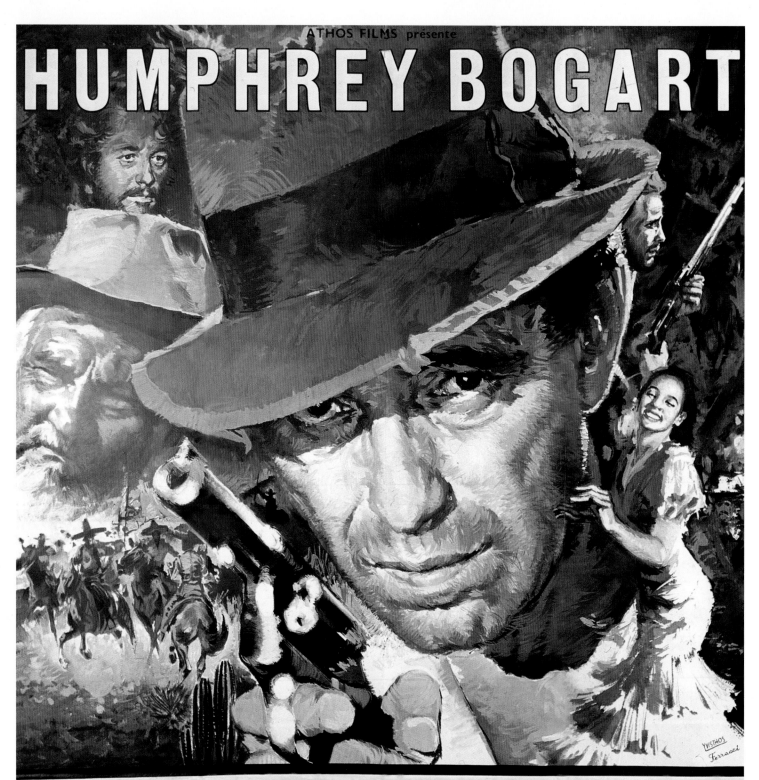

ATHOS FILMS présente

HUMPHREY BOGART

LE TRESOR DE LA
SIERRA MADRE

WALTER HUSTON • **TIM HOLT** • **BRUCE BENNET**
SCÉNARIO DE JOHN HUSTON D'APRÈS LA NOUVELLE DE B.TRAVEN . MUSIQUE DE MAX STEINER
MISE EN SCÈNE DE

PRODUIT PAR
HENRY BLANKE
JOHN HUSTON

Bogart on Broadway and Filmography

On Broadway

Drifting by John Colton, D.H. Andrews
Producer: William A. Brady
Director: John Cromwell
with Alice Brady, H. Mortimer White
Playhouse (January 22) 1922

Up the Ladder by Owen Davis
Producer: William A. Brady
Director: Lumsden Hare
with George Farren, Nanette Comstock, Doris Kenyon
Playhouse (March 6) 1922

Swifty by John Peter Toohey, W.C.Percival
Producer: William A. Brady
Director: John Cromwell
with Frances Howard, Hale Hamilton, William Holden
Playhouse (October 16) 1922

Meet the Wife by Lynn Starling
Producers: Rosalie Stewart, Bert Fench
Director: Bert French
with Mary Boland, Charles Dalton, Eleanor Griffith, Clifton Webb
Klaw (November 26) 1923

Nerves by John Farrar, Stephen Vincent Benét
Producer: William A. Brady
Director: William A. Brady Jr.
with Marie Curtis, Kenneth MacKenna, Paul Kelly, Mary Philips
Comedy (September 1) 1924

Hell's Bells by Barry Connors
Producer: Herman Gantvoort
Director: John Hayden
with Olive May, Shirley Booth, Tom H.Walsh
Wallack's (January 26) 1925

Cradle Snatchers by Russell Medcraft, Norma Mitchell
Producer: Sam H. Harris
Director: Sam Forrest with Mary Boland, Edna May Oliver, Margaret Dale, Myra Hampton
Music Box (September 7) 1925

Saturday's Children by Maxwell Anderson
Director: Guthrie McClintic
with Ruth Hammond, Richard Barbee, Lucia Moore, Ruth Gordon
Booth (January 26) 1927

Baby Mine by Margaret Mayo
Director: John Turekwith Roscoe "Fatty" Arbuckle, Lee Patrick
Bogart took over role from Roger Pryor
Chanin's 46th Street (June 9) 1927

A Most Immoral Lady by Townsend Martin
Producers: William A. Brady Jr., Dwight Deere Wiman
Director: Dwight Deere Wiman with Alice Brady
Bogart took over unlisted role
Cort (November 26) 1928

The Skyrocket by Mark Reed
Producers: Gilbert Miller, Guthrie McClintic
with Mary Philips (as Phillips), J.C. Nugent, Clara Blandick
Lyceum (January 11) 1929

It's a Wise Child by Laurence E. Johnson
Producer/Director: David Belasco
with Helen Lowell, Olga Krolow, Leile Bennett, George Walcott
Belasco (August 6) 1929

After All by John Van Druten
Producer: Dwight Deere Wiman
Director: Auriol Lee
with Helen Haye, Walter Kingsford, Edmund George, Margaret Perry
Booth (December 3) 1931

I Loved You Yesterday by Molly Ricardel, William Du Bois
Producer: Crosby Gaige
Director: Worthington Miner
with Frances Fuller, Edward La Roche, Henry O'Neill, Jane Seymour
Sam H. Harris (October 11) 1932

Chrysalis by Rose Albert Porter
Producer: Martin Beck
Director: Theresa Helburn
with Lily Cahill, Osgood Perkins, Margaret Sullavan, Gilbette Frey, Fran Bourke, Elisha Cook Jr.
Martin Beck (November 15) 1932

Our Wife by Lillian Day, Lyon Mearson
Producers: Thomas J.R. Brotrherton, Abe H. Halle
Director: Edward Clarke Lilley
with Rose Hobart, June Walker
Booth (March 2) 1932

The Mask and the Face by Luigi Chiarelli,
translated from Italian by W. Somerset Maugham
Producer: Theatre Guild
Director: Philip Moeller
with Shirley Booth, Donald McClelland, Dorothy Patten, Leo G. Carroll
Guild (May 8) 1932

Invitation to a Murder by Rufus King
Producer: Ben Stein
Director: A.H. Van Buren
with William Valentine, Daphne Warren Wilson, James Shelburne, Gale Sondergaard
Masque (May 17) 1932

The Petrified Forest by Robert E. Sherwood
Producers: Gilbert Miller, Leslie Howard
Director: Arthur Hopkins
with Leslie Howard, Peggy Conklin, Charles Dow Clark, Frank Milan, Walter Vonnegut, Blanche Sweet
Broadhurst (January 7) 1935

Filmography

Up the River (Fox) 92 minutes
Director: John Ford
Screenplay: Maurine Dallas Watkins
Cinematographer: Joseph August
Cast: Spencer Tracy (St. Louis); Claire Luce (Judy); Warren Hymer (Dannemora Dan); Humphrey Bogart (Steve); William Collier Sr. (Pop); Joan Marie Lawes (Jean); George MacFarlane (Jessup); Gaylord Pendleton (Morris)
Opened October 10, 1930 *see page 96*

A Devil With Women (Fox) 76 minutes
Director: Irving Cummings
Screenplay: Dudley Nichols, Henry M. Johnson from novel Dust and Sun by Clements Ripley
Cinematography: Arthur Todd
Cast: Victor McLaglen (Jerry Maxton); Mona Maris (Rosita Fernadez); Humphrey Bogart (Tom Standish); Luana Alcañiz (Dolores); Michael Vavitch (Morloff); Soledas Jiménez (Jimimez); Mona Rico (Alicia); John St Polis (Don Diego); Robert Edeson (General Garcia)
Opened October 18, 1930 *see page 96*

Body and Soul (Fox) 70 minutes
Director: Alfred Santell
Screenplay: Jukes Furthman from play Squadrons by Elliott White Springs, A. E. Thomas based on story by Elliott White Springs
Cinematographer: Glen MacWilliams
Cast: Charles Farrell (Mal Andrews); Elissa Landi (Carla); Myrna Loy (Alice Lester); Humphrey Bogart (Jim Watson); Donal Dillaway (Tap Johnson); Crauford Kent (Major Burke); Pat Somerset (Major Knowles); Ian Maclaren (General Trafford-Jones)
Opened February 22, 1931 *see page 97*

Bad Sister (Universal) 68 minutes
Director: Hobart Henley
Screenplay: Raymond L. Schrock, Tom Reed, dialogue Edwin H. Knopf from story by Booth Tarkington
Cinematography: Karl Freund
Cast: Bette Davis (Laura Madison); Conrad Nagel (Dick Lindley); Sidney Fox (Marianne Madison); ZaSu Pitts (Minnie); Slim Summerville (Sam); Charles Winninger (John Madison); Emma Dunn (Mrs Madison); Humphrey Bogart (Valentine Corliss)
Opened March 29, 1931 *see page 99*

Women of all Nations (Fox) 72 minutes
Director: Raoul Walsh
Screenplay: Barry Conners, based on characters created by Laurence Stallings and Maxwell Anderson
Cinematography: Lucien Andriot
Cast: Victor McLaglen (Sergeant Flagg); Edmund Lowe (Sergeant Quirt); El Brendel (Olson); Greta Nissen (Elsa); Fifi Dorsay (Fifi); Marjorie White (Pee Wee); T. Roy Barnes (Captain of Marines); Bela Lugosi (Prince Hassan); Humphrey Bogart (Stone); Joyce Compton (Kiki)
Opened May 31, 1931 *see page 99*

A Holy Terror (Fox) 53 minutes
Director: Irving Cummings
Screenplay: Ralph Block from novel *Trailin'* by Max Brand
Cinematography: George Schneiderman
Cast: George O'Brien (Tony Bard); Sally Eilers (Jerry Foster); Rita La Roy (Kitty Carroll); Humphrey Bogart (Steve Nash); James Kirkood (William Drew); Stanley Fields (Butch Morgan)
Opened July 19, 1931 *see page 99*

Love Affair (Columbia) 68 minutes
Director: Thornton Freeland
Screenplay: Jo Swerling, based on story by Ursula Parrott
Cinematography: Ted Tetzlaff
Cast: Dorothy Mackaill (Carol Owen); Humphrey Bogart (Jim Leonard); Jack Kennedy (Gilligan); Barbara Leonard (Felice); Astrid Allwyn (Linda Lee); Bradley Page (Georgie); Halliwell Hobbes (Kibbee)
Opened March 17, 1932 *see page 99*

Big City Blues (Warner) 65 minutes
Director: Mervyn LeRoy
Screenplay: Ward Morehouse, Lillie Hayward from play *New York Town* by Ward Morehouse
Cinematography: James Van Trees
Cast: Joan Blondell (Vida Fleet); Eric Linden (Bud Reeves); Jobyna Howland (Serena Carlich); Inez Courtney (Faun); Evelyn Kanpp (JoJo); Guy Kibbee (Hummel); Gloria Shea (Agnes); Walter Catlett (Gibboney); Ned Sparks (Stackhouse); Humphrey Bogart (Shep Adkins); Lyle Talbot (Sully); Josephine Dunne (Jackie); Grant Mitchell (Station Agent)
Opened September 10, 1932 *see page 99*

Three On a Match (Warner) 64 minutes
Director: Mervyn LeRoy
Screenplay: Lucien Hubbard, Kubec Glasmon, John Bright
Cinematography: Sol Polito
Cast: Joan Blondell (Mary Keaton); Warren William (Robert Kirkwood); Ann Dvorak (Vivian Revere); Bette Davis (Ruth Wescott); Lyle Talbot (Michael Loftus); Humphrey Bogart (Harve); Allen Jenkins (Dick); Edward Arnold (Ace); Grant Mitchell (Mr. Gilmore); Glenda Farrell (Prisoner); Frankie Darro (Bobby)
Opened October 28, 1932 *see page 99*

Midnight (All-Star/Universal) 76 minutes
Producer/director: Chester Erskine
Screenplay: Chester Erskine based on play by Paul and Clair Sifton
Cinematography: William Steiner, George Webber
Cast: Sidney Fox (Stella Weldon); O. P. Heggie (Edward Weldon); Henry Hull (Bob Nolan); Margaret Wycherly (Mrs Weldon); Lynne Overmann (Joe "Leroy" Biggers); Katherine Wilkson (Ada Biggers); Richard Whorf (Arthur Weldon); Humphrey Bogart (Garboni); Cora Witherspoon (Elizabeth McGrath); Moffat Johnson (District Attorney Plunkett)
Opened March 7, 1934 *see page 99*

The Petrified Forest (Warner) 83 minutes
Director: Archie Mayo
Screenplay: Charles Kenyon, Delmer Daves from play by Robert E. Sherwood
Cinematography: Sol Polito
Cast: Leslie Howard (Alan Squier); Bette Davis (Gabrielle Maple); Genevieve Tobin (Mrs Edith Chisholm); Dick Foran (Boze Hertzlinger); Humphrey Bogart (Duke Mantee); Joseph Sawyer (Jackie); Porter Hall (Jason Maple); Charles Grapewin (Gramp Maple); Paul Harvey (Mr Chisholm); Eddie Acuff (Lineman)
Opened February 6, 1936 *see page 102*

Bullets or Ballots (Warner/First National) 81 minutes
Director: William Keighley
Screenplay: Seton I. Miller, based on story by Martin Mooney and Seton I. Miller
Cinematography: Hal Mohr
Cast: Edward G. Robinson (Johnny Blake); Joan Blondell (Lee Morgan); Barton MacLane (Al Kruger); Humphrey Bogart (Nick "Bugs" Fenner); Frank McHugh (Herman McKloske); Joseph King (Captain Dan McLaren); Richard Purcell (Ed Driscoll); George E. Stone (Wires Kagel); Joseph Crehan (Grand Jury Spokesman); Henry O'Neill (Ward Bryant); Henry Kolker (Hollister); Gilbert Emery (Thorndyke); Herbert Rawlinson (Caldwell); Louise Beavers (Nellie); William Pawley (Crail)
Opened June 6, 1936 *see page 105*

Two Against the World (Warner/First National) 64 minutes
Director: William McGann
Screenplay: Michael Jacoby, based on play *Five Star Final* by Louis Wetzenkorn
Cinematography: Sid Hickox
Cast: Humphrey Bogart (Sherry Scott); Beverly Roberts (Alma Ross); Henry O'Neill (Jim Carstairs); Linda Perry (Edith Carstairs); Carlyle Moore Jr. (Billy Sims); Virginia Brissac (Mrs Marion Sims); Helen MacKellar (Martha Carstairs); Clay Clement (Mr. Banning); Claire Dodd (Cora Latimer); Hobart Cavanaugh (Tippy Mantus)
Opened July 11, 1936 *see page 105*

China Clipper (Warner/First National) 85 minutes
Director: Ray Enright
Screenplay: Frank Ward, additional dialogue Norman Reilly Raine
Cinematography: Arthur Edeson
Cast: Pat O'Brien (Dave Logan); Beverly Roberts (Jean Logan); Ross Alexander (Tom Collins); Humphrey Bogart (Hap Stuart); Marie Wilson (Sunny Avery); Joseph Crehan (Jim Horn); Joseph King (Mr. Pierson); Addison Richards (B. C. Hill); Ruth Robinson (Mother Brunn); Henry B. Walthall (Dad Brunn); Carlyle Moore Jr. (Radio Operator); Lyle Moraine (Co-pilot); Dennis Moore (Engineer); Wayne Morris (Navigator); Alexander Cross (Bill Andrews)
Opened August 11, 1936 *see page 105*

Isle of Fury (Warner) 60 minutes
Director: Frank L. McDonald
Screenplay: Robert Andrews, Robert Jacobs, based on novel *Narrow Corner* by W. Somerset Maugham
Cinematography: Frank Good
Cast: Humphrey Bogart (Val Stephens); Margaret Lindsay (Lucille Gordon); Donald Woods (Eric Blake); Paul Graetz (Captain Deever); Gordon Hart (Anderson); E. E. Clive (Dr. Hardy); George Regas (Otar); Sidney Bracy (Sam); Tetsu Komai (Kim Lee); Miki Morita (Oh Kay)
Opened October 10, 1936 *see page 105*

Black Legion (Warner) 83 minutes
Director: Archie Mayo
Screenplay: Abem Finkel, William Wister Haines from story by Robert Lord
Cinematography: George Barnes
Cast: Humphrey Bogart (Frank Taylor); Dick Foran (Ed Jackson); Erin Brian Moore (Ruth Taylor); Ann Sheridan (Betty Grogan); Robert Barrat (Brown); Helen Flint (Pearl Davis); Joseph Sawyer; Addison Richards (Prosecuting Attorney); Eddie Acuff; Clifford Soubier (Mike Grogan)
Opened January 17, 1937 *see page 106*

The Great O'Malley (Warner) 71 minutes
Director: William Dieterle
Screenplay: Milton Krims, Tom Reed, based on story by Gerald Beaumont
Cinematography: Ernest Haller
Cast: Pat O'Brien (James Aloysius O'Malley); Sybil Jason (Barbra Phillips); Humphrey Bogart (John Phillips); Ann Sheridan (Judy Nolan); Frieda Inescourt (Mrs Phillips); Donald Crisp (Captain Cromwell); Henry O'Neill (Defense Attorney); Craig Reynolds (Motorist); Hobart Cavanaugh (Pinky); Gordon Hart (Doctor); Mary Gordon (Mrs O'Malley)
Opened February 13, 1937 *see page 106*

Marked Woman (Warner/First National) 96 minutes
Director: Lloyd Bacon
Screenplay: Robert Rossen, Abem Finkel
Cinematography: George Barnes
Cast: Bette Davis (Mary Dwight Strauber); Humphrey Bogart (David Graham); Lola Lane (Gabby Marvin); Eduardo Ciannelli (Johnny Vanning); Rosalind Marquis (Florrie Liggett); Mayo Methot (Estelle Potter); Jane Bryan (Betty Strauber); Allen Jenkins (Louie); John Litel (Gordon); Ben Welden (Charlie Delaney); Damian O'Flynn (Ralph Krawford); Henry O'Neill (Arthur Sheldon)
Opened April 10, 1937 *see page 106*

Kid Galahad (Warner) 102 minutes
Director: Michael Curtiz
Screenplay: Seto I. Miller, based on novel by Francis Wallace
Cinematography: Tony Gaudio
Cast: Edward G. Robinson (Nick Donati); Bette Davis (Fluff); Humphrey Bogart (Turkey Morgan); Wayne Morris (Ward Guisenberry); Jane Bryan (Marie Donati); Harry Carey (Silver Jackson); Willian Haade (Chuck McGraw); Soledad Jiminez (Mrs Donati); Joe Cunningham (Joe Taylor); Ben Welden (Buzz Barett); Joseph Crehan (Brady); Veda Ann Borg (Redhead)
Opened May 26, 1937 *see page 106*

San Quentin (Warner/First National) 70 minutes
Director: Lloyd Bacon
Screenplay: Peter Milne, Humphrey Cobb, based on story by Robert Tasker and John Bright
Cinematography: Charlie Hickox
Cast: Pat O'Brien (Captain Stephen Jameson); Humphrey Bogart (Joe "Red" Kennedy); Ann Sheridan (May Kennedy); Barton MacLane (Captain Druggin); Joseph Sawyer (Sailor Boy Hansen); Veda Ann Borg (Helen); James Robbins (Mickey Callahan); Joseph King (Warden Taylor); Gordon Oliver (Captain); Garry Owen (Dopey); Marc Lawrence (Venetti)
Opened August 3, 1937 *see page 106*

Dead End (United Artists) 93 minutes
Director: William Wyler
Screenplay: Lillian Hellman, based on play by Sidney Kingsley
Cinematography: Gregg Toland
Cast: Sylvia Sidney (Drina Gordon); Joel McCrea (Dave Connell); Humphrey Bogart (Baby Face Martin); Wendy Barrie (Kay Burton); Claire Trevor (Francey); Allen Jenkins (Hunk); Marjorie Main (Mrs Martin); Billy Halop (Tommy); Huntz Hall (Dippy); Bobby Jordan (Angel); Leo Gorcey (Spit); Gabriel Dell (T. B.); Bernard Punsley (Milty); Charles Peck (Philip Griswold); Minor Watson (Mr. Griswold); Ward Bond (Doorman)
Opened August 24, 1937 *see page 111*

Stand-In (Walter Wanger/United Artists) 91 minutes
Director: Tay Garnett
Screenplay: Gene Towne, Graham Baker based on story by Clarence Budington Kelland
Cinematography: Charles Clarke
Cast: Leslie Howard (Atterbury Dodd); Joan Blondell (Lester Plum); Humphrey Bogart (Douglas Quintain); Alan Mowbray (Koslofski); Marle Shelton (Thelma Cheri); C. Henry Gordon (Ivor Nassau); Jack Carson (Potts); Tully Marshall (Fowler Pettypacker); J. C. Nugent (Pettypacker Junior); William V. Mong (Cyrus Pettypacker); Art Baker (Director of Photography); Charles Middleton (Abe Lincoln Actor); Esther Howard (Landlady); Olin Howard (Hotel Manager); Pat Flaherty (Nightclub Bouncer)
Opened October 29, 1937 see page 111

Swing Your Lady (Warner) 80 minutes
Director: Ray Enright
Screenplay: Joseph Schrank, Maurice Leo based on play by Kenyon Nicholson and Charles Robinson
Cinematographer: Arthur Edeson
Cast: Humphrey Bogart (Ed Hatch); Frank McHugh (Popeye Bronson); Louise Fazenda (Sadie Horn); Nat Pendleton (Joe Skopapoulos); Penny Singleton (Cookie Shannon); Allen Jenkins (Shiner Ward); Leon Weaver (Waldo Davis); Frank Weaver (Ollie Davis); Elviry Weaver (Mrs Davis); Ronald Reagan (Jack Miller); Daniel Boone Savage (Noah Webster); Hugh O'Connell (Smith)
Opened January 8, 1938 see page 111

Crime School (Warner/First National) 85 minutes
Director: Lewis Seiler
Screenplay: Crane Wilbur, Vincent Sherman from story by Crane Wilbur
Cinematography: Arthur Todd
Cast: Humphrey Bogart (Mark Braen); Gale Page (Sue Warren); Billy Halop (Frankie Warren); Huntz Hall (Goofy); Leo Gorcey (Spike Hawkins); Bernard Punsley (Fats Papadopoulos); Gabriel Dell (Bugs Burke); George Offerman Jr. (Red); Weldo Heyburn (Cooper); Cy Kendall (Morgan); Charles Trowbridge (Judge Clinton); Spencer Charters (Old Doctor); Donald Briggs (New Doctor); Frank Jacquet (Commissioner)
Opened May 10, 1938 see page 111

Men Are Such Fools (Warner) 69 minutes
Director: Busby Berkeley
Screenplay: Norman Reilly Raine, Horace Jackson based on novel by Faith Baldwin
Cinematography: Sid Hickox
Cast: Wayne Morris (Jimmy Hall); Priscilla Lane (Linda Lawrence); Humphrey Bogart (Henry Galleon); Hugh Herbert (Harvey Bates); Penny Singleton (Nancy); Johnnie Davis (Tad); Mona Barrie (Beatrice Harris); Marcia Ralston (Wanda Townsend); Gene Lockhart (Bill Dalton); Kathleen Lockhart (Mrs Dalton); Carole Landis (Jill Cooper)
Opened June 15, 1938 see page 111

Racket Busters (Warner/Cosmopolitan) 71 minutes
Director: Lloyd Bacon
Screenplay: Robert Rossen, Leonardo Bercovici
Cinematography: Arthur Edeson
Cast: Humphrey Bogart (Pete Martin); George Brent (Denny Jordan); Gloria Dickson (Nora Jordan); Allen Jenkins (Horse Wilson); Walter Abel (Thomas Allison); Henry O'Neill (Governor); Penny Singleton (Gladys); Anthony Averill (Crane); Oscar O'Shea (Pop Wilson)
Opened July 16, 1938 see page 112

The Amazing Dr. Clitterhouse (Warner/First National) 87 minutes
Director: Anatole Litvak
Screenplay: John Wexley, John Huston based on play by Barré Lyndon
Cinematographer: Tony Gaudio
Cast: Edward G. Robinson (Dr. Clitterhouse); Claire Trevor (Jo Keller); Humphrey Bogart (Rocks Valentine); Allen Jenkins (Okay); Donald Crisp (Inspector Lane); Gale Page (Nurse Randolph); Henry O'Neill (Judge); John Litel (Prosecuting Attorney); Thurston Hall (Grant); Maxie Rosenbloom (Butch); Bert Hanlon (Pal); Curt Bois (Rabbit); Ward Bond (Tug)
Opened July 20, 1938 see page 112

Angels With Dirty Faces (Warner/First National) 97 minutes
Director: Michael Curtiz
Screenplay: John Wexley, Warren Duff from story by Rowland Brown
Cinematography: Sol Polito
Cast: James Cagney (Rocky Sullivan); Pat O'Brien (Jerry Connolly); Humphrey Bogart (James Frazier); Ann Sheridan (Laury Ferguson); George Bancroft (Mac Keefer); Billy Halop (Soapy); Bobby Jordan (Swing); Leo Gorcey (Bim); Gabriel Dell (Patsy); Huntz Hall (Crab); Bernard Punsley (Hunky); Joseph Downing (Steve); Edward Pawley (Edwards); Adrian Morris (Blackie)
Opened November 24, 1938 see page 112

King of the Underworld (Warner) 69 minutes
Director: Lewis Seiler
Screenplay: George Bricker, Vincent Sherman from story by W. R. Burnett
Cinematography: Sid Hickox
Cast: Humphrey Bogart (Joe Gurney); Kay Francis (Dr. Carol Nelson); James Stephenson (Bill Stevens); John Eldedge (Dr. Niles Nelson); Jessie Busley (Aunt Margaret); Arthur Aylesworth (Dr. Sanders); Raymond Brown (Sheriff); Harland Tucker (Mr. Ames); Ralph Remley (Mr. Robert); Charley Foy (Slick); Murray Alper (Eddie); Joe Devlin (Porky); Elliott Sullivan (Mugsy); Alan Davis (Pete); John Jarmon (Slats); John Ridgely (Jerry); Richard Quine (Student)
Opened January 7, 1939 see page 116

The Oklahoma Kid (Warner) 89 minutes
Director: Lloyd Bacon
Screenplay: Warren Duff, Robert Bruckner, Edward E. Paramore based on story by Edward E. Paramore and Wally Klein
Cinematography: James Wong Howe
Cast: James Cagney (Jim Kincaid); Humphrey Bogart (Whip McCord); Rosemary Lane (Jane Hardwick); Donald Crisp (Judge Hardwick); Hugh Sothern (John Kincaid); Harry Stephens (Ned Kincaid); Charles Middleton (Alec Martin); Edward Pawley (Doolin); Ward Bond (Wes Handley); Irving Bacon (Hotel Clerk); Joe Devlin (Keely); Wade Boteler (Sheriff Abe Collins)
Opened March 3, 1939 see page 116

You Can't Get Away With Murder
(Warner/First National) 79 minutes
Director: Lewis Seiler
Screenplay: Robert Buckner, Don Ryan, Kenneth Gamet based on play *Chalked Out* by Warden Lewis and Jonathan Finn
Cinematography: Sol Polito
Cast: Humphrey Bogart (Frank Wilson); Billy Halop (Johnnie Stone); Gale Page (Madge Stone); John Litel (Attorney Carey);

Henry Travers (Pop); Harvey Stephens (Fred Burke); Harold Hubba (Scrapper); Joseph Sawyer (Red); Joseph Downing (Smitty); George E. Stone (Toad); Joseph King (Principal Keeper); Joseph Crehan (Warden); John Ridgely (Gas Station Attendant); Herbert Rawlinson (District Attorney)
Opened March 24, 1939 see page 116

Dark Victory (Warner) 105 minutes
Director: Edmund Goulding
Screenplay: Casey Robinson based on play by George Emerson Brewer Jr. and Bertram Bloch
Cinematographer: Ernest Haller
Cast: Bette Davis (Judith Trahearne); George Brent (Dr. Frederick Steele); Humphrey Bogart (Michael O'Leary); Geraldine Fitzgerald (Ann King); Ronald Reagan (Alec Hamm); Henry Travers (Dr. Parsons); Cora Witherspoon (Carrie Spottswood); Dorothy Peterson (Miss Wainwright); Virginia Brissac (Martha)
Opened April 20, 1939 see page 116

The Roaring Twenties (Warner) 104 minutes
Director: Raoul Walsh
Screenplay: Jerry Wald, Richard Macaulay, Robert Rossen based on story by Mark Hellinger
Cinematography: Ernest Haller
Cast: James Cagney (Eddie Bartlett); Priscilla Lane (Jean Sherman); Humphrey Bogart (George Hally); Gladys George (Panama Smith); Jeffrey Lynn (Lloyd Hart); Frank McHugh (Danny Green); Paul Kelly (Nick Brown); Elisabeth Risdon (Mrs Sherman); Edward Keane (Pete Henderson); Joe Sawyer (Sergeant Pete Jones); Joseph Crehan (Mr. Fletcher); George Meeker (Masters); John Hamilton (Judge)
Opened October 23, 1939 see page 119

The Return of Dr. X (Warner/First National) 62 minutes
Director: Vincent Sherman
Screenplay: Lee Katz, based on story by William J. Makin
Cinematography: Sid Hickox
Cast: Humphrey Bogart (Marshall Quesne/Dr. Xavier); Wayne Morris (Walter Barnett); Rosemary Lane (Joan Vance); Dennis Morgan (Dr. Michael Rhodes); John Litel (Dr. Francis Flegg); Lya Lys (Angela Merrova); Huntz Hall (Pinky); Charles Wilson (Detective Ray Kincaid)
Opened November 23, 1939 see page 119

Invisible Stripes (Warner) 81 minutes
Director: Lloyd Bacon
Screenplay: Warren Duff, from story by Jonathan Finn, based on book by Warden Lewis E. Lawes
Cinematography: Ernest Haller
Cast: George Raft (Cliff Taylor); Jane Bryan (Peggy); William Holden (Tim Taylor); Humphrey Bogart (Chuck Martin); Flora Robson (Mrs Taylor); Paul Kelly (Ed Kruger); Lee Patrick (Molly); Henry O'Neill (Parole Officer Masters); Frankie Thomas (Tommy); Moroni Olsen (Warden); Margot Stevenson (Sue); Marc Lawrence (Lefty); Joseph Downing (Johnny); Leo Gorcey (Jimmy)
Opened December 30, 1939 see page 119

Virginia City (Warner) 121 minutes
Director: Michael Curtiz
Screenplay: Robert Buckner
Cinematography: Sol Polito
Cast: Errol Flynn (Kerry Bradford); Miriam Hopkins (Julia Hayne); Randolph Scott (Vance Irby); Humphrey Bogart (John Murrell); Frank McHugh (Mr. Upjohn); Alan Hale (Olaf "Moose"

Swenson); Guinn "Big Boy" Williams (Marblehead); John Litel (Marshall); Douglas Dumbrille (Major Drewery); Moroni Olsen (Dr. Cameron); Russell Hicks (Armistead); Dickie Jones (Cobby)
Opened March 16, 1940 *see page 123*

It All Came True (Warner/First National) 97 minutes
Director: Lewis Seiler
Screenplay: Michael Fessier, Lawrence Kimble based on story by Louis Bromfield
Cinematography: Ernest Haller
Cast: Ann Sheridan (Sarah Jane Ryan); Jeffrey Lynn (Tommy Taylor); Humphrey Bogart (Grasselli/Chips Maguire); ZaSu Pitts (Miss Flint); Una O'Connor (Maggie Ryan); Jessie Busley (Norah Taylor); John Litel (Mr. Roberts); Grant Mitchell (Mr. Salmon); Felix Bressart (Mr. Boldini); Charles Judels (Leantopulos)
Opened April 6, 1940 *see page 123*

Brother Orchid (Warner) 88 minutes
Director: Lloyd Bacon
Screenplay: Earl Baldwin, based on story by Richard Connell
Cinematography: Tony Gaudio
Cast: Edward G. Robinson (Little John Sarto); Ann Sothern (Flo Adams); Humphrey Bogart (Jack Buck); Donald Crisp (Brother Superior); Ralph Bellamy (Clarence Fletcher); Allen Jenkins (Willie the Knife); Charles D. Brown (Brother Wren); Cecil Kellaway (Brother Goodwin); Morgan Conway (Philadelphia Powell); Richard Lane (Mugsy O'Day); Paul Guilfoyle (Red Martin); John Ridgely (Texas Pearson); Joseph Crehan (Brother MacEwen); Wilfred Lucas (Brother MacDonald); Tom Tyler (Curley Matthews); Dick Wessel (Buffalo Burns)
Opened June 7, 1940 *see page 123*

They Drive By Night (Warner) 95 minutes
Director: Raoul Walsh
Screenplay: Jerry Wald, Richard Macaulay, based on novel *Long Haul* by A. I. Bezzerides
Cinematography: Arthur Edeson
Cast: George Raft (Joe Frabrini); Ann Sheridan (Cassie Hartley); Ida Lupino (Lana Carlsen); Humphrey Bogart (Paul Fabrini); Gale Page (Pear Fabrini); Alan Hale (Ed Carlsen); Roscoe Karns (Irish McGurn); John Litel (Harry McNamara); George Tobias (George Rondolos); Henry O'Neill (District Attorney); Paul Hurst (Pete Haig); Charles Halton (Fransworth); John Ridgely (Hank Dawson); George Lloyd (Barney); Joyce Compton (Sue Carter)
Opened July 27, 1940 *see page 123*

High Sierra (Warner/First National) 100 minutes
Director: Raoul Walsh
Screenplay: John Huston, W. R. Burnett, based on novel by W. R. Burnett
Cinematography: Tony Gaudio
Cast: Ida Lupino (Marie Garson); Humphrey Bogart (Roy Earle); Alan Curtis (Babe Kozak); Arthur Kennedy (Red Hatter); Joan Leslie (Velma); Henry Hull (Doc Banton); Barton MacLane (Jake Kranmer); Henry Travers (Pa Goodhue); Elisabeth Risdon (Ma Goodhue); Jerome Cowan (Healy); Cornel Wilde (Louis Mendoza); Minna Gombell (Mrs Baughman); Paul Harvey (Mr. Baughman); John Eldredge (Lon Preiser); Donald MacBride (Big Mac); Isabel Jewell (Blonde); Willie Best (Algernon); Spencer Charters (Ed); George Meeker (Pfiffer); Robert Strange (Art); Sam Hayes (Announcer); Arthur Aylesworth (Auto Court Owner); Wade Boteler (Sheriff); Erville Alderson (Farmer); Eddy Chandler (Policeman)
Opened January 21, 1941 *see page 124*

The Wagons Roll at Night (Warner/First National)
84 minutes
Director: Ray Enright
Screenplay: Fred Niblo Jr., Barry Trivers from novel *Kid Galahad* by Francis Wallace
Cinematography: Sid Hickox
Cast: Humphrey Bogart (Nick Coster); Sylvia Sidney (Flo Lorraine); Eddie Albert (Matt Varney); Joan Leslie (Mary Coster); Sig Rumann (Hoffman the Great); Cliff Clark (Doc); Charley Foy (Snapper); Frank Wilcox (Tex); John Ridgely (Arch); Clara Blandwick (Mrs Williams); Aldrich Bowker (Mr. Williams); Garry Owen (Gus); Jack Mower (Bundy); Frank Mayo (Wally)
Opened April 25, 1941 *see page 124*

The Maltese Falcon (Warner/First National) 101 minutes
Director: John Huston
Screenplay: John Huston, based on novel by Dashiell Hammett
Cinematography: Arthur Edeson
Cast: Humphrey Bogart (Sam Spade); Mary Astor (Brigid O'Shaughnessy); Gladys George (Iva Archer); Peter Lorre (Joel Cairo); Barton MacLane (Lieutenant Dundy); Lee Patrick (Effie Perine); Sydney Greenstreet (Casper Guttman); Ward Bond (Detective Tom Polhaus); Jerome Cowan (Miles Archer); Elisha Cook Jr. (Wilmer Cook); James Burke (Luke); Murray Alper (Frank Richman); John Hamilton (District Attorney Bryan); Emory Parnell (Mate of La Paloma); Walter Huston (Captain Jacobi)
Opened October 3, 1941 *see page 126*

All Through the Night (Warner/First National)
107 minutes
Director: Vincent Sherman
Screenplay: Leonard Spigelglass, Edwin Gilbert Based on original story by Leonard Q. Ross [Leo Rosten]
Cinematography: Sid Hickox
Cast: Humphrey Bogart (Gloves Donahue); Conrad Veidt (Hal Ebbing); Kaaren Verne (Leda Hamilton); Jane Darwell (Ma Donahue); Frank McHugh (Barney); Peter Lorre (Pepi); Judith Anderson (Madama); William Demarest (Sunshine); Jackie Gleason (Starchy); Phil Silvers (Waiter); Wallace Ford (Spats Hunter); Barton MacLane (Marty Callahan); Edward Brophy (Joe Denning); Martin Kosleck (Steindorff); Jean Ames (Annabelle); Ludwig Stossel (Mr. Miller); Irene Seidner (Mrs Miller); James Burkes (Forbes); Ben Welden (Smitty); Hans Schumm (Anton); Charles Cane (Spence); Frank Sully (Sage); Sam McDaniel (Deacon)
Opened January 23, 1942 *see page 130*

The Big Shot (Warner/First National) 82 minutes
Director: Lewis Seiler
Screenplay: Bertram Millhauser, Abem Finkel, Daniel Fuchs
Cinematography: Sid Hickox
Cast: Humphrey Bogart (Duke Berne); Irene Manning (Lorna Fleming); Richard Travis (George Anderson); Susan Peters (Ruth Carter); Stanley Ridges (Martin Fleming); Minor Watson (Warden Booth); Chick Chandler (Dancer); Joseph Downing (Frenchy); Howard da Silva (Sandor); Murray Alper (Quinto); Roland Drew (Faye); John Ridgely (Tim); Joseph King (Toohey); John Hamilton (Judge); Virginia Brissas (Mrs Booth); William Edmund (Sarto); Virginia Sale (Mrs Miggs); Ken Christy (Kat); Wallace Scott (Rusty)
Opened June 13, 1942 *see page 130*

Across the Pacific (Warner/First National) 97 minutes
Director: John Huston (final scenes Vincent Sherman)
Screenplay: Richard Macaulay
Cinematography: Arthur Edeson

Cast: Humphrey Bogart (Richard Thomas Leland); Mary Astor (Alberta Marlow); Sydney Greenstreet (Dr. Lorenz); Charles Halton (A. V. Smith); Victor Sen Young (Joe Totsukio); Roland Got (Sugi); Lee Tung Foo (Sam Wing On); Frank Wilcox (Captain Morrison); Paul Stanton (Colonel Hart); Lester Matthews (Canadian Major); John Hamilton (Court-martial President); Tom Stevenson (Tall Thin Man); Roland Drew (Captain Harkness); Monte Blue (Dan Morton); Chester Gan (Captain Higoto)
Opened September 4, 1942 *see page 130*

Casablanca (Warner/First National) 102 minutes
Director: Michael Curtiz
Screenplay: Julius and Philip Epstein, Howard Koch based on play *Everybody Comes to Rick's* by Murray Burnett and Joan Alison
Cinematography: Arthur Edeson
Cast: Humphrey Bogart (Richard Blaine); Ingrid Bergman (Ilsa); Paul Henreid (Victor Laszlo); Claude Rains (Captain Louis Renault); Conrad Veidt (Major Heinrich Strasser); Sydney Greenstreet (Ferrari); Peter Lorre (Ugarte); S. Z. Sakall (Carl); Madeleine LeBeau (Yvonne); Dooley Wilson (Sam); Joy Page (Annina Brandel); John Qualen (Berger); Leonid Kinsky (Sascha); Helmut Dantine (Jan Brandel); Curt Bois (Pickpocket); Marcel Dalio (Emil)
Opened November 26, 1942 *see page 132*

Action in the North Atlantic (Warner/First National)
126 minutes
Director: Lloyd Bacon
Screenplay: John Howard Lawson, A. I. Bezzerides, W. R. Burnett based on novel by Guy Gilpatric
Cinematography: Ted McCord
Cast: Humphrey Bogart (First Mate Joe Rossi); Raymond Massey (Captain Steve Jarvis); Alan Hale (Boats O'Hara); Julie Bishop (Pearl); Ruth Gordon (Mrs Jarvis); Sam Levene (Chips Abrams); Dane Clark (Johnny Pulaski); Peter Whitney (Whitey Lara); Dick Hogan (Cadet Robert Parker); Minor Watson (Rear Admiral Hartridge); J. M. Kerrigan (Caviar Jinks); Kane Richmond (Ensign Wright); William von Brincken (U-boat Captain); Chick Chandler (Goldberg); George Offerman Jr. (Cecil); Don Douglas (Lieutenant Commander); Art Foster (Pete Larson); Ray Montgomery (Aherne); Glenn Strange (Tex Matthews); Creighton Hale (Sparks); Elliott Sullivan (Hennessy); Alec Craig (McGonigle); Ludwig Stossel (Captain Ziemer); Dick Wessel (Cherub); Frank Puglia (Captain Carpolis); Iris Adrian (Jenny O'Hara); Irving Bacon (Bartender); James Flavin (Lieutenant Commander)
Opened May 21, 1943 *see page 138*

Thank Your Lucky Stars (Warner/First National)
124 minutes
Director: David Butler
Screenplay: Norman Panama, Melvin Frank, James V. Kern based on story by Everett Freeman and Arthur Schwartz
Cinematography: Arthur Edeson
Stars as themselves: Humphrey Bogart, Eddie Cantor, Bette Davis, Olivia de Havilland, Errol Flynn, John Garfield, Joan Leslie, Ida Lupino, Ann Sheridan, Dinah Shore, Alexis Smith, Jack Carson, Alan Hale, George Tobias etc
Opened October 1, 1943 *see page 138*

Sahara (Columbia) 97 minutes
Director: Zoltan Korda
Screenplay: John Howard Lawson, Zoltan Korda based on story by Philip MacDonald from Soviet film *The Thirteen*
Cinematographer: Rudolph Maté
Cast: Humphrey Bogart (Sergeant Joe Dunn); Bruce Bennett

(Waco Hoyt); J. Carroll Naish (Giuseppe); Lloyd Bridges (Fred Clarkson); Rex Ingram (Tambul); Richard Nugent (Captain Jason Halliday); Dan Duryea (Jimmy Doyle); Carl Harbord (Marty Williams); Patrick O'Moore (Ozzie Bates); Louis Mercier (Jean Leroux); Guy Kingsford (Peter Stegman); Kurt Kreuger (Captain Von Schletow); John Wengraf Major Von Falken); Hans Schumm (Sergeant Krause); Frank Lackteen (Arab Guide)
Opened October 14, 1943 see page 138

Passage to Marseille (Warner/First National)
109 minutes
Director: Michael Curtiz
Screenplay: Casey Robinson, Jack Moffit based on novel Men Without Country by Charles Nordhof and James Norman Hall
Cinematography: James Wong Howe
Cast: Humphrey Bogart (Matrac); Claude Rains (Captain Freycinet); Michele Morgan (Paula); Philip Dorn (Renault); Sydney Greenstreet (Major Duval); Peter Lorre (Marius); George Tobias (Petit); Helmut Dantine (Garou); John Loder (Manning); Victor Francen (Captain Malo); Vladimir Sokoloff (Grandpere)
Opened February 16, 1944 see page 138

To Have and Have Not (Warner/First National)
100 minutes
Producer/director: Howard Hawks
Screenplay: Jules Furthmann, William Faulkner from novel by Ernest Hemingway
Cinematography: Sid Hickox
Cast: Humphrey Bogart (Harry "Steve" Morgan); Walter Brennan (Eddie); Lauren Bacall (Marie "Slim" Browning); Dolores Moran (Helene de Brusac); Hoagy Carmichael (Cricket); Walter Molnar (Paul de Brusac); Sheldon Leonard (Lieutenant Coyo); Marcel Dalio (Gerard); Walter Sande (Johnson); Dan Seymour (Captain Renard); Aldo Nadi (Renard's Bodyguard); Paul Marion (Beauclerc); Patricia Shay (Mrs Beauclerc)
Opened October 11, 1944 see page 140

Conflict (Warner/First National) 86 minutes
Director: Curtis Bernhardt
Screenplay: Arthur T. Horman, Dwight Taylor based on original story by Robert Siodmak and Alfred Neumann
Cinematography: Merritt Gerstad
Cast: Humphrey Bogart (Richard Manson); Alexis Smith (Evelyn Turner); Sydney Greenstreet (Dr. Mark Hamiliton); Rose Hobart (Kathryn Mason); Charles Drake (Professor Norman Holdsworth); Grant Mitchell (Dr. Grant); Patrick O'Moore (Detective Lieutenant Egan); Ann Shoemaker (Nora Grant); Frank Wilcox (Robert Freston); Edwin Stanley (Phillips)
Opened June 15, 1945 see page 140

Two Guys from Milwaukee (Warner/First National)
90 minutes
Director: David Butler
Screenplay: Charles Hoffman, I. A. L. Diamond
Cinematography: Arthur Edeson
Cast: Dennis Morgan (Prince Henry); Joan Leslie (Connie Reed); Janis Paige (Polly); S. Z. Sakall (Count Oswald); Patti Brady (Peggy); Tom D'Andrea (Happy); Rosemary DeCamp (Nan); John Ridgely (Mike Collins); Pat McVey (Johnson); Franklin Pangborn (Theater Manager); Francis Pierlot (Dr. Bauer); Lauren Bacall (Herself); Humphrey Bogart (Himself)
Opened July 26, 1946 see page 140

The Big Sleep (Warner/First National) 114 minutes
Producer/director: Howard Hawks
Screenplay: William Faulkner, Leigh Brackett, Jules Furthmann

from novel by Raymond Chandler
Cinematography: Sid Hickox
Cast: Humphrey Bogart (Philip Marlowe); Lauren Bacall (Vivian Rutledge); John Ridgely (Eddie Mars); Martha Vickers (Carmen Sternwood); Dorothy Malone (Acme Bookstore Proprietress); Peggy Knudsen (Mona Mars); Regis Toomey (Bernie Ohls); Charles Waldron (Genberal Sternwood); Charles D. Brown (Norris); Bob Steele (Canino); Elisha Cook Jr. (Harry Jones); Louis Jean Heydt (Joe Brody)
Opened August 23, 1946 see page 142

Dead Reckoning (Columbia) 100 minutes
Director: John Cromwell
Screenplay: Oliver H. P. Garrett, Steve Fisher, adapted by Allen Rivkin from story by Gerald Adams and Sidney Biddell
Cinematography: Leo Tover
Cast: Humphrey Bogart (Rip Murdock); Lizabeth Scott (Coral Chandler); Morris Carnovsky (Martinelli); Charles Caner (Lieutenant Kincaid); William Prince (Johnny Drake); Marvin Miller (Krause); Wallace Ford (McGee); James Bell (Father Logan); George Chandler (Louis Ord); William Forrest (Lieutenant-Colonel Simpson); Ruby Dandridge (Hyacinth)
Opened January 2, 1947 see page 146

The Two Mrs. Carrolls (Warner/First National)
99 minutes
Director: Peter Godfrey
Screenplay: Thomas Job, based on play by Martin Vale
Cinematography: Peverell Marley
Cast: Humphrey Bogart (Geoffrey Carroll); Barbara Stanwyck (Sally Carroll); Alexis Smith (Cecily Latham); Nigel Bruce (Dr. Tuttle); Isobel Elsom (Mrs Latham); Patrick O'Moore (Charles Pennington); Ann Carter (Beatrice Carroll); Anita Bolster (Christine); Barry Bernard (Mr. Blagdon); Colin Campbell (MacGregor)
Opened March 4, 1947 see page 146

Dark Passage (Warner/First National) 106 minutes
Director: Delmer Daves
Screenplay: Delmer Daves based on novel by David Goodis
Cinematography: Sid Hickox
Cast: Humphrey Bogart (Vincent Parry); Lauren Bacall (Irene Jansen); Bruce Bennett (Bob Rapf); Agnes Moorehead (Madge Rapf); Tom D'Andrea (Sam); Clifton Young (Baker); Douglas Kennedy (Detective); Rory Mallinson (George Fellsinger); Houseley Stevenson (Dr. Walter Coley)
Opened September 5, 1947 see page 146

Always Together (Warner/First National) 78 minutes
Director: Frederick de Cordova
Screenplay: Phoebe and Henry Ephron, I. A. L. Diamond
Cinematography: Carl Guthrie
Cast: Robert Hutton (Donn Masters); Joyce Reynolds (Jane Barker); Cecil Kellaway (Jonathan Turner); Ernest Truex (Mr. Bull); Donn McGuire (McIntyre); Ransom Sherman (Judge); Douglas Kennedy (Doberman); Humphrey Bogart (Himself)
Opened December 10, 1947 see page 146

The Treasure of the Sierra Madre (Warner/First National)
126 minutes
Director: John Huston
Screenplay: John Huston, from novel by B. Traven
Cinematography: Ted McCord
Cast: Humphrey Bogart (Fred C. Dobbs); Walter Huston (Howard); Tim Holt (Curtin); Bruce Bennett (Cody); Barton MacLane McCormick); Alfonso Bedoya (Gold Hat); A. Sango

Ragel (Presidente); Manuel Donde (El Jefe); Jose Torvay (Pablo); Margarito Luna (Pancho); Jacqueline Dalya (Flashy Girl); Robert Blake (Lottery Ticket Boy); John Huston (American in White Suit)
Opened January 6, 1948 see page 148

Key Largo (Warner/First National) 101 minutes
Director: John Huston
Screenplay: John Huston, Richard Brooks, based on play by Maxwell Anderson
Cinematography: Karl Freund
Cast: Humphrey Bogart (Frank McCloud); Edward G. Robinson (Johnny Rocco); Lauren Bacall (Nora Temple); Lionel Barrymore (James Temple); Claire Trevor (Gaye Dawn); Thomas Gomez (Curley Hoff); Harry Lewis (Toots Bass); John Rodney (Deputy Clyde Sawyer); Marc Lawrence (Ziggy); Dan Seymour (Angel Garcia); Monte Blue (Sherif Ben Wade); William Haade (Ralph Feeney); Jay Silverheels (John Osceola); Roderick Redwing (Tom Osceola)
Opened July 16, 1948 see page 152

Knock On Any Door (Santana/Columbia) 100 minutes
Director: Nicholas Ray
Screenplay: Daniel Taradash, John Monks Jr. based on novel by William Motley
Cinematography: Burnett Guffey
Cast: Humphrey Bogart (Andrew Morton); John Derek (Nick Romano); George Macready (Kerman); Allene Roberts (Emma); Susan Perry (Adele Morton); Mickey Knox (Vito); Barry Kelley (Judge Drake)
Opened February 21, 1949 see page 158

Tokyo Joe (Santana/Columbia) 88 minutes
Director: Stuart Heisler
Screenplay: Cyril Hume, Bertram Millhauser, adapted by Walter Doniger from story by Steve Fisher
Cinematography: Charles Lawton Jr.
Cast: Humphrey Bogart (Joe Barrett); Alexander Knox (Mark Landis); Florence Marley (Trina); Sessue Hayakawa (Baron Kimura); Jerome Courtland (Danny); Gordon Jones (Idaho); Teru Shimada (Ito); Hideon Mori (Kanda); Charles Meredith (General Ireton); Rhys Williams (Colonel Dahlgren); Lora Lee Michael (Anya)
Opened October 26, 1949 see page 158

Chain Lightning (Warner/First National) 94 minutes
Director: Stuart Heisler
Screenplay: Liam O'Brien, Vincent Evans based on story by J. Redmond Prior
Cinematography: Ernest Haller
Cast: Humphrey Bogart (Matt Brennan); Eleanor Parker (Jo Holloway); Raymond Massey (Leland Wallis); Richard Whorf (Carl Troxell); James Brown (Major Hinkle); Roy Roberts (General Hewitt); Morris Ankrum (Ed Bostwick); Fay Barker (Mrs Willis); Fred Sherman (Jeb Farley)
Opened February 18, 1950 see page 164

In a Lonely Place (Santana/Columbia) 94 minutes
Director: Nicholas Ray
Screenplay: Andrew Solt, adapted by Edmund North from novel by Dorothy Hughes
Cinematography: Burnett Guffey
Cast: Humphrey Bogart (Dixon Steele); Gloria Grahame (Laurel Gray); Frank Lovejoy (Brub Nicolai); Carl Benton Reid (Captain Lochner); Art Smith (Mel Lippman); Jeff Donnell (Sylvia Nicolai); Martha Stewart (Mildred Atkinson); Robert Warwick (Charlie Waterman); Morris Ankrum (Lloyd Barnes); William Ching (Ted

Barton); Steven Geray (Paul); Hadda Brooks (Singer); Alix Talton (Frances Randolph); Jack Reynolds (Henry Kesler); Ruth Warren (Effie); Ruth Gillette (Martha); Guy Beach (Swan); Lewis Howard (Junior)
Opened May 17, 1950 *see page 164*

The Enforcer (United States/Warner) 87 minutes
Director: Bretaigne Windust
Screenplay: Martin Rackin
Cinematography: Robert Burks
Cast: Humphrey Bogart (Martin Ferguson); Zero Mostel (Big Babe Lazich); Ted de Corsia (Joseph Rico); Everett Sloane (Albert Mendoza); Roy Roberts (Captain Frank Nelson); Lawrence Tolan (Duke Malloy); King Donovan (Sergeant Whitlow); Bob Steele (Herman); Adelaide Klein (Olga Kirshen); Don Beddoe (Thomas O'Hara); Tito Vuelo (Tony Vetto); John Kellogg (Vince); Jack Lambert (Philadelphia Tom Zaca)
Opened January 25, 1951 *see page 164*

Sirocco (Santana/Columbia) 98 minutes
Director: Curtis Bernhardt
Screenplay: A. I. Bezzerides, Hans Jacoby based on novel *Coup de Grâce* by Joseph Kessel
Cinematography: Burnett Guffey
Cast: Humphrey Bogart (Harry Smith); Marta Toren (Violette); Lee J. Cobb (Colonel Feroud); Everett Sloane (General LaSalle); Gerald Mohr (Major Leaon); Zero Mostel (Balukjian); Nick Dennis (Nasir Aboud); Onslow Stevens (Emir Hassan); David Bond (Achmet); Ludwig Donath (Flophouse Proprietor); Vincent Renno (Arthur)
Opened June 1, 1951 *see page 165*

The African Queen (Horizon/Romulus, United Artists)
105 minutes, Technicolor
Director: John Huston
Screenplay: James Agee, John Huston from novel by C. S. Forester
Cinematography: Jack Cardiff
Cast: Humphrey Bogart (Charlie Allnut); Katharine Hepburn (Rose Sayer); Robert Morley (Rev Samuel Sayer); Peter Bull (Louisa Captain); Theodore Bikel (Louisa First Officer); Walter Gotell (Louisa Second Officer); Gerald Onn (Louisa Petty Officer); Peter Swanwick (Shona First Officer); Richard Marner (Shona Second Officer)
Opened December 23, 1951 *see page 166*

Deadline – U.S.A. (Twentieth Century-Fox) 87 minutes
Director: Richard Brooks
Screenplay: Richard Brooks
Cinematography: Milton Krasner
Cast: Humphrey Bogart (Ed Hutchinson); Ethel Barrymore (Mrs John Garrison); Kim Hunter (Nora); Ed Begley (Frank Allen); Warren Stevens (George Burrows); Paul Stewart (Harry Thompson); Martin Gabel (Thomas Reinzi); Joe De Santis (Herman Schmidt); Joyce MacKenzie (Kitty Garrison Geary); Audrey Christy (Mrs Willebrandt); Fay Baker (Alice Garrison Courtenay); Jim Backus (Jim Cleary)
Opened March 14, 1952 *see page 171*

Road to Bali (Paramount) 91 minutes, Technicolor
Director: Hal Walker
Opened November 19, 1952

Battle Circus (Metro-Goldwyn-Mayer) 90 minutes
Director: Richard Brooks
Screenplay: Richard Brooks, based on story by Allen Rivkin and Laura Kerr
Cinematography: John Alton
Cast: Humphrey Bogart (Major Jed Webbe); June Allyson (Lieutenant

Ruth McCara); Keenan Wynn (Sergeant Orvil Statt); Robert Keith (Lieutenant Colonel Hilary Walters); William Campbell (Captain John Rustford); Perry Sheehan (Lieutenant Lawrence); Patricia Tiernan (Lieutenant Rose Ashland); Jonathan Cott (Adjutant); Adele Longmire (Lieutenant Jane Franklin); Ann Morrison (Lieutenant Edith Edwards); Helen Winston (Lieutenant Graciano); Sarah Selby (Captain Dobbs); Danny Chang (Danny); Philip Ahn (Korean Prisoner); Steve Forrest (Sergeant)
Opened March 6, 1953 *see page 171*

Beat the Devil (Santana-Romulus/United Artists)
93 minutes
Director: John Huston
Screenplay: John Huston, Truman Capote based on novel by James Helvick (Claud Cockburn)
Cinematography: Oswald Morris
Cast: Humphrey Bogart (Billy Dannreuther); Jennifer Jones (Gwendolen Chelm); Gina Lollobrigida (Maria Dannreuther); Robert Morley (Petersen); Peter Lorre (O'Hara); Edward Underdown (Harry Chelm); Ivor Barnard (Major Ross); Bernard Lee (Jack Clayton, CID Inspector); Marco Tulli (Ravello); Mario Perroni (Purser); Alex Pochet (Hotel Manager); Aldo Silvani (Charles); Giulio Donnini (Administrator); Saro Uzi (Captain); Juan de Landa (Hispano-Suiza Driver); Manuel Serano (Arab Officer); Mimo Poli (Barman)
Opened November 24, 1953 *see page 171*

The Love Lottery (Ealing/Rank) 89 minutes, Technicolor
Director: Charles Crichton
Opened January 1954 *see page 171*

The Caine Mutiny (Stanley Kramer/Columbia)
125 minutes, Technicolor
Director: Edward Dmytryk
Screenplay: Stanley Roberts, Michael Blankfort from novel by Herman Wouk
Cinematography: Franz Planer
Cast: Humphrey Bogart (Captain Philip Francis Queeg); José Ferrer (Lieutenant Barney Greenwald); Van Johnson (Lieutenant Steve Maryk); Fred MacMurray (Lieutenant Tom Keefer); Robert Francis (Ensign Willie Keith); May Wynn (May Wynn); Tom Tully (Lieutenant Commander DeVries); E. G. Marshall (Lieutenant Commander Challee); Arthur Franz (Lieutenant Paynter); Lee Marvin (Meatball); Warner Anderson (Captain Blakely); Claude Akins (Horrible); Katharine Warren (Mrs Keith); Jerry Paris (Ensign Harding); Steve Brodie (Chief Budge)
Opened June 24, 1954 *see page 172*

Sabrina (Paramount) 113 minutes
Director: Billy Wilder
Screenplay: Billy Wilder, Samuel Taylor, Ernest Lehman from play *Sabrina Fair* by Samuel Taylor
Cinematography: Charles Lang Jr.
Cast: Humphrey Bogart (Linus Larrabee); Audrey Hepburn (Sabrina Fairchild); William Holden (David Larrabee); Walter Hampden (Walter Larrabee); John Williams (Thomas Fairchild); Martha Hyer (Elizabeth Tyson); Joan Vohs (Gretchen Van Horn); Marcel Dalio (Baron); Marcel Hillaire (The Professor); Nella Walker (Maude Larrabee); Francis X. Bushman (Mr. Tyson); Ellen Corby (Miss McCardle); Marjorie Bennett (Margaret the Cook); Emory Parnell (Charles the Butler); Kay Riehl (Mrs Tyson); Nancy Kulp (Jenny the Maid)
Opened September 9, 1954 *see page 174*

The Barefoot Contessa (Figaro. United Artists)
128 minutes, Technicolor
Director: Joseph L. Mankiewicz
Screenplay: Joseph L. Mankiewicz
Cinematography: Jack Cardiff
Cast: Humphrey Bogart (Harry Dawes); Ava Gardner (Maria

Vargas); Edmond O'Brien (Oscar Muldoon); Marius Goring (Alberto Bravanao); Valentina Cortesa (Eleanora Torlato-Favrini); Rosanno Brazzi (Vincenzo Torlato-Favrini); Elizabeth Sellars (Jerry); Warren Stevens (Kirk Edwards); Franco Interlenghi (Pedro); Mari Aldon (Myrna); Bessie Love (Mrs Eubanks); Diana Decker (Drunken Blonde); Bill Fraser (J. Montague Brown); Alberto Rabagliati (Nightclub Owner); Enzo Staiola (Busboy)
Opened September 29, 1954 *see page 174*

We're No Angels (Paramount)
103 minutes, Technicolor VistaVision
Director: Michael Curtiz:
Screenplay: Ranald MacDougall from play *La Cuisine des Anges* by Albert Husson
Cinematography: Loyal Griggs
Cast: Humphrey Bogart (Joseph); Aldo Ray (Albert); Peter Ustinov (Jules); Joan Bennett (Amelie Ducotel); Basil Rathbone (Andre Tochard); Leo G. Carroll (Felix Ducotel); John Baer (Paul Trochard); Gloria Talbott (Isabelle Ducotel); Lea Penman (Madame Parole); John Smith (Arnaud); Louis Mercier (Celeste); George Dee (Coachman); Torben Meyer (Butterfly Man); Paul Newlan (Port Captain); Ross Gould (Foreman)
Opened July 7, 1955 *see page 176*

The Left Hand of God (Twentieth Century-Fox)
87 minutes, Technicolor CinemaScope
Director: Edward Dmytryk
Screenplay: Alfred Hayes based on novel by William E. Barrett
Cinematography: Franz Planer
Cast: Humphrey Bogart (Jim Carmody); Gene Tierney (Anne Scott); Lee J. Cobb (Mieh Yang); Agnes Moorehead (Beryl Sigman); E. G. Marshall (Dr. David Sigman); Jean Porter (Mary Yin); Carl Benton Reid (Reverend Cornelius); Victor Sen Young (John Wong); Benson Fong (Chun Tien); Richard Cutting (Father O'Shea); Leon Lonto (Pao Ching); Don Forbes (Father Keller)
Opened September 21, 1955 *see page 176*

The Desperate Hours (Paramount) 112 minutes, VistaVision
Director: William Wyler
Screenplay: Joseph Hayes based on his novel and play
Cinematography: Lee Garmes
Cast: Humphrey Bogart (Glenn Griffin); Fredric March (Dan Hiliard); Arthur Kennedy (Jesse Bard); Martha Scott (Eleanor Hilliard); Dewey Martin (Hal Griffin); Gig Young (Chuck); Mary Murphy (Cindy Hilliard); Richard Eyer (Ralphie Hilliard); Robert Middleton (Sam Kobish); Alan Reed (Detective); Bert Freed (Winston); Ray Collins (Masters); Whit Bissell (Carson); Ray Teal (Fredericks)
Opened October 5, 1955 *see page 178*

The Harder They Fall (Columbia) 109 minutes
Director: Mark Robson
Screenplay: Philip Yordan based on novel by Budd Schulberg
Cinematography: Burnett Guffey
Cast: Humphrey Bogart (Eddie Willis); Rod Steiger (Nick Benko); Jan Sterling (Beth Willis); Mike Lane (Toro Moreno); Max Baer (Buddy Brannan); Jersey Joe Wolcott (George); Edward Andrews (Jim Weyerhause); Harold J Stone (Art Leavitt); Carlos Montalban (Luis Agrandi); Nehemiah Persoff (Leo); Felice Orlandi (Vince Fawcett); Herbie Fay (Max); Rusty Lane (Danny Mckeogh); Jack Albertson (Pop)
Opened May 9, 1956 *see page 179*

Select Bibliography

Bacall, Lauren
By Myself and Then Some, Alfred A. Knopf, New York, 2005

Barbour, Alan G.
Humphrey Bogart, Galahad Books, New York, 1973

Benchley, Nathaniel
Humphrey Bogart, Little Brown, Boston, 1975

Bogart, Stephen
Bogart: In Search of My Father, Dutton, New York, 1995

Coe, Jonathan
Humphrey Bogart: Take It and Like It, Bloomsbury, London, 1991

Eisenschnitz, Bernard
Humphrey Bogart, Le Terrain Vague, Paris, 1967

Eyles, Allen
Bogart, Macmillan, London, 1975

Gehman, Richard
Bogart: An Intimate Biography, Fawcett-Gold Medal, New York, 1965

Goodman, Ezra
Bogey: The Good-Bad Guy, Lyle Stuart, New York, 1965

Hyams, Joe
Bogie, New American Library, New York, 1966

McCarty, Clifford
Bogey: The Films of Humphrey Bogart, Citadel Press, New York, 1965

Meyers, Jeffrey
Bogart: A Life in Hollywood, Houghton Mifflin, New York, 1997

Michael, Paul
Humphrey Bogart The Man and His Films, Bonanza Books, New York, 1965

Pettigrew, Terrence
Bogart: A Definitive Study of His Film Career, Proteus, New York, 1981

Ruddy, Jonah & Hill, Jonathan
Bogey: The Man, the Actor, the Legend, Tower, New York, 1965

Sperber, A. M. & Lax, Eric
Bogart, William Morrow, New York, 1997

Picture Credits

The Estate of Humphrey Bogart: *10*

Corbis: *22*

The Kobal Collection: *1, 2 Columbia/Bob Coburn, 5, 6 Warner Bros., 9, 14, 17 Warner Bros., 18 Columbia, 21, 24, 26 Warner Bros., 29, 33 Warner Bros./First National, 34 Warner Bros./First National, 36–37 Warner Bros./First National, 39 Warner Bros., 41 Warner Bros., 42 Warner Bros., 45 Warner Bros., 48 Warner Bros., 51 Warner Bros., 52 Warner Bros., 55, 56–57 Warner Bros./John Engstead, 58 Warner Bros., 61, 63, 64 Warner Bros., 67 Columbia/Bob Coburn, 69 United Artists, 70 United Artists, 73 Columbia, 74–75 Paramount, 78, 80 Warner Bros., 85, 88, 91 Vitaphone, 92 Warner Bros., 95 Warner Bros., 96 Fox Films, 97 Fox Films, 98t Universal, 98b Columbia, 100–101 Columbia, 103 Warner Bros., 104t First National, 104b Warner Bros., 107 Warner Bros./Bert Longworth, 108–109 Goldwyn/United Artists, 110 Warner Bros., 113 Warner Bros./First National, 114–115 Warner Bros./First National, 117 Warner Bros., 118 Warner Bros./First National, 123 Warner Bros., 125 Warner Bros./First National, 126 Warner Bros./First National, 127 Warner Bros./First National, 128–129 Warner Bros./First National, 131 Warner Bros./First National, Warner Bros., 133 Warner Bros., 134t Warner Bros., 134b Warner Bros., 135t Warner Bros., 135b Warner Bros., 136–137 Warner Bros., 139t Warner Bros., 139b Columbia/Ned Scott, 140 Warner Bros./Mac Julian, 141 Warner Bros., 142 Warner Bros., 143 Warner Bros./John Engstead, 144 Warner Bros.,, 145t Warner Bros., 145b Warner Bros., 147 Warner Bros., 149 Warner Bros., 150–151 Warner Bros., 152 Warner Bros., 153 Warner Bros., 154–155 Warner Bros., 156 Warner Bros., 157t Warner Bros., 157b Warner Bros., 159 Columbia, 160 20th Century Fox, 163 Columbia, 165 Columbia/Irving Lippman, 166 United Artists, 167 United Artists, 168–169 United Artists, 170t 20th Century Fox, 170b MGM, 172 Columbia, 173 Columbia, 174 Paramount, 175 United Artists, 176 Paramount, 177 20th Century Fox, 178 Paramount, 179 Columbia, 180, 183 Warner Bros./Scotty Welbourne, 184 Warner Bros., 191 Warner Bros.,*

MPTV.net: *12-13 Sid Avery, 30, 77 John Swope, 120 Warner Bros*

The nature of photography within the Hollywood studio system was that many publicity stills were released for free editorial use with the associated photographic credits not provided. We would be pleased to rectify any omissions or inaccuracies in future editions.